Food from *FINLAND*

ANNA-MAIJA AND JUHA TANTTU

Food from FINLAND

HELSINGISSÄ
KUSTANNUSOSAKEYHTIÖ OTAVA

Sixth edition

Copyright © 1988 by Anna-Maija and Juha Tanttu
Translated by Martha Gaber Abrahamsen
Captions by Juha Tanttu and Clayton Andrews
Lay-out by Jukka Mäkelä

Acknowledgements: We would like to thank the following
companies for their support. We are gratetul for the
illustrations and recipes they have provided: ALKO Oy
Ab, Elintarviketeollisuusliitto, Leipätoimikunta, Martta-
liitto ry, Matkailun edistämiskeskus MEK, Raision
Yhtymä, Suomen Sokeri Oy/Vaasan Mylly, Tapolan
Palvaamo Oy, Valio Meijerien Keskusosuusliike.

Anna-Maija Tanttu received a grant from Suomen
Kulttuurirahasto/ Hotelli-ja ravintolaneuvosto ry. for this
book.

Printed in Keuruu, Finland

Otava Publishing Company Printing Plant
Keuruu, 1994

ISBN 951-1-10121-8

Contents

Finland — a Few Facts 6
The Land of Four Gastronomic Seasons 9
   Springtime — Great Expectations 10
   Well Worth Fishing — and Eating 13
   Summertime — and the Night is White 21
   The Night of the Crayfish 27
   Autumn Leaves and Mushrooms 30
   Winter Darkness — Christmas Lights 37
Where and What to Eat 46
The Smörgåsbord, "voileipäpöytä," is a Finnish
Banquet 51
Local Delicacies 56
Some Specialities 64
The Eating Day 67
   Morning 67
   Noon 68
   Dinner and Supper 69
   Tea and Sandwiches 70
   Dessert 71
   Excellent Cheese 74
   Invitation to a Sauna 76
A Country of Black Bread 79
Pastries, Pasties, and Pies 82
A Cup of Coffee? 87
When You're Thirsty 88
Some Habits of Your Hosts 91
What to Bring Home 92
Index 94
Weights and Measures 96

Finland —
a Few Facts

Finland is an Arctic country: a fourth of its area lies north of the Arctic Circle. The Gulf Stream, though, makes Finland warmer than, for example, northern Siberia, Alaska, and southern Greenland, which lie just as far north.

The Finns like to say that they live in a small country, but they're too modest as Finland is the seventh largest country in Europe. But Finland is proud of its 60.000 lakes.

Finland's temperature in July usually ranges from 13 to 20°C, but the mercury can soar to over 30°. In February, the range is from –3 to –14°C, but the thermometer can drop to –30°C. Autumn is the rainiest season.

The winter brings snow and darkness. Northern Finland gets its snow cover in October or November, while the rest of the country has to wait till as late as December. The snow usually melts in April, but in Lapland it can stay until June.

The shortest winter day in southern Finland lasts six hours, the longest summer day about 19. Lapland has its "nightless nights" in June and July, but in the deep of winter, the sun doesn't rise for almost two months.

Finland has five million inhabitants, with an average of 15 Finns to the sq. km. Half of the population lives in the south, though, in only a tenth of the total area. The move to the south is continuing, and so is urbanization in general. The life expectancy of Finnish men is roughly 71 years, while Finnish women can expect to live eight years longer.

A few Finns have won international renown: Alvar Aalto, the architect; Jean Sibelius, the composer; Urho Kekkonen, Finland's president for a quarter of a century; Paavo Nurmi and Lasse Virén, the Olympic runners; Timo Mäkinen, Ari Vatanen, and Juha Kankkunen, the rally drivers; designer Timo Sarpaneva; and conductors Esa-Pekka Salonen and Jukka-Pekka Saraste.

The Finnish language belongs to the Fenno-Ugric linguistic family, as do Estonian and Hungarian. Almost 6% of all Finns speak Swedish as their native tongue instead of Finnish.

Finland has been an independent republic since 1917. From 1809 until independence, it had been an autonomous Grand Duchy of Russia, and before that, part of the Kingdom of Sweden.

"Finland would be a wonderful country – if it weren't for the climate and the people . . ." That was probably said tongue in cheek by someone who wanted to keep away swarms of tourists in order to enjoy this far-off corner of Europe and its unusual inhabitants all by himself.

The climate is what makes Finland what it is. Finland without the four clearly marked seasons would not be Finland. It's a ridiculous idea: just ask any Finn. For the Finn, you see, is always waiting for the next season. No matter what the weather is like, a change is always in store and is always welcome.

This is true of food, too. There is a kind of hysterical feeling of anticipation for the treats of the next season: the roe season, the strawberry season, the mushroom season. . . It has been said that there are at least four reasons for visiting Finland: winter, spring, summer, and autumn, and every season of the year has its own foods.

Lately, there have been two clear trends in Finnish cuisine. More attention is paid to elegance and simplicity. Today something akin to Japanese aesthetics and perhaps also *la Nouvelle Cuisine Française* influence the way food is served, the way tables are set, complementing the practicality that has always been typical of Finnish design.

The second key trend is attention to proper nutrition. Finland is a land of cardiovascular diseases, but for some time now, doctors have urged the Finns to eat foods with less fat. And the Finns have listened. The campaign for less fat and the availability the year round of more fruits and vegetables imported or grown in Finnish greenhouses have helped reduce cardiovascular disease. It's gotten to the point where some gourmets actually long for the bad old days of greasy meat!

If you're looking for something special and exotic then try reindeer meat, the staple of the Lapps. There are lots of ways of serving reindeer, but one of the most popular with natives and tourists alike is *Reindeer stew*. All you need is a chunk of frozen reindeer meat, butter or pork fat (Don't worry, Doctor. Reindeer is lean!), some snow to cook with, and a proper Arctic setting. The result will be a memorable meal!

Some things, like reindeer meat, are specialties of the far north. But other delicacies have come from West and East — Sweden and Russia, and even France, by way of the Russian court in St. Petersburg. The French influence can still be found, and one visiting French chef à la mode, noting similarities and differences, remarked, ''I hope you Finns realize what wonderful eating opportunities you have, with the four seasons and all the delicious and natural ingredients. . .''

We do, and so will our visitors! Bon appetit!

The Land
of Four Gastronomic Seasons

Finnish products come fresh from the fields, forests, and waters.

Springtime — Great Expectations

Springtime. March, April, May. A time when the Finns march along muddy roads in rubber boots, spread evergreen branches before their front steps, watch the return of the birds from the south — and await the summer. Faces turn toward the sun, which bakes them brown, reflected by the snow. Everyone has a good appetite on a spring day like this.

Housewives examine their cupboards and freezers: the last jams from last summer, juices and other preserves are put on the table. This is the time when the first Finnish cucumbers, tomatoes, and radishes reach the stores — expensive but wonderful! Last season's potatoes begin to shrivel and sprout. And so the wait for summer is also the wait for good, new potatoes.

The spring's bright spot is Easter. Children color eggs, decorate the table with special things, put pussy willows in vases. Treats abound, and one of the truly gourmet delicacies is the *Mignon egg* — a real eggshell filled with the finest chocolate nougat.

There are many traditional Easter foods. Some dishes came from the east along with the Orthodox church: *pasha, baba, kulitsa.* People eat lamb. And there is *mämmi,* a sweet baked malt dish, for dessert.

The snow begins to melt and the ice disappears from the lakes. The sun gets warmer and houses look dingy in its bright light. The windows just have to be washed.

Boats are made shipshape.

Finland's answer to the carnival is Vappu — May Day — which starts the evening before, on the 30th of April, Walpurgis Night. May Day is always a spring day, if only because the Finns have decided it is, in spite of the fact that this is when the season's last sleet always seems to fall. May Day is a workers' and students' holiday: red flags, white student caps, streamers, balloons, noise, singing, restaurants filled to the brim. Many families and friends gather year after year on May Day at the same time and same place. And everyone makes merry.

Traditional May Day foods are *tippaleipä,* deep-fried cookies that resemble fantastic bird's nests, and *sima,* mead. Herring and icy schnapps are a must for May Day morning.

One of the great joys of spring is looking for morels, *korvasieni.* These crumpled ball-like

Sima
Mead

5 l water
2 lemons
1/4 kg granulated sugar
1/4 kg brown sugar
2 dl syrup
1/4 tsp fresh yeast or a pinch of dried yeast
(1 bottle of beer)

Into the bottles:
raisins and sugar

1. Peel the lemons (preferably unsprayed — otherwise well scrubbed!) with a potato peeler, taking off the rind. Then remove and discard the white layer and cut the lemon and peel into slices.
2. Place the lemon and sugar into a large bowl.
3. Bring the water to a boil and pour it over the other ingredients.
4. Let the mixture cool, and when it is lukewarm, add the yeast, dissolved in a bit of liquid.
5. Let the mead ferment at room temperature overnight.
6. Pour through a sieve and bottle it. Put a few raisins and a teaspoon of sugar in each bottle before closing.
7. Keep the bottles at room temperature for a few hours, and then store in a cool place.
8. The drink is ready to serve after a few days, but is best in a week.

Finnish doughnuts are often round, at their best freshly baked, and sprinkled with sugar.

Tippaleivät
May Day cookies

2 eggs
2 tsp sugar
1 tsp salt
2 dl milk
4 dl flour
1/2 tsp vanillin

To fry:
vegetable or coconut oil

1. Mix the eggs and sugar, but don't beat! Add the other ingredients and stir into a smooth batter.
2. Put the batter into a paper cone or a pastry bag fitted with a small-holed nozzle.
3. Squeeze the batter in a thin band into the hot oil. Use a spiral motion to form nest-like cookies. If possible, use a metal ring in the pot to keep the cookies in shape.
4. When the cookies have turned golden brown, remove and drain them on paper towels.
5. Dust the cold cookies with powdered sugar.

Pikamunkit
Quick doughnuts

5 dl flour
1/2 dl sugar
1 tsp salt
3 tsp baking powder
2 tsp cardamom
3 dl top milk or light cream
2 eggs

1. Mix the dry ingredients in a bowl.
2. Add the milk/cream and eggs. Mix into a smooth dough.
3. Take small dabs of dough and drop them immediately into hot oil (180°C). Cook until light brown, about 4—5 minutes.
4. Roll in sugar while still warm and serve as soon as possible.

mushrooms are a seasonal delicacy, and even a few will please the mushroom hunter, whose own special patches are guarded secrets. The mushrooms are dried or thoroughly boiled to remove the poison. They're creamed and eaten as such or with small potatoes, bacon, beef, or salmon. Gastronomical gold.

Spring hasn't come until the ice cream stands have appeared on street corners and in parks in every Finnish town. Summer is here when you can see the long but patient line waiting in front of the ice cream stand at the railway station or in front of the local athletic field.

Ice cream. Of course. Finland *is* a big dairy producer. The tradition of making ice cream came all the way from Italy, partly via St. Petersburg. Product development and the Finn's enthusiasm for the sweet and unusual have created new kinds of ice cream, whole new products. Ice cream, which originally really did mark the beginning of a new season, has for years been a year-round treat, a popular dessert and favorite way of pacifying children.

The Finns love to gorge on vanilla ice cream. If the occasion is especially important one can always top it with strawberry jam or — on even more festive occasions — cloudberry jam.

The Finn is irritated by the foreign conception that Finland is a cold country where Eskimos roam the streets. The truth is that *Finns* roam the streets — in summer eating Eskimo pies to ward off the heat!

The lakes are finally free of ice, with the last bits dissolving as ice-cubes do in a glass left to sit. The fish begin to live again, splash and spawn.

And here we have a paradox: when the water is coldest, many of the fish are at their most passionate. The result is roe — Ah! say the gourmets — and in time, a lot more fish.

The Finns of yesteryear didn't know anything about nutrition, but they did know how good fish are. Fish were eaten bones and all, and this is one way the Finns got their calcium and trace elements.

Another old tradition is eating fish raw. Finland is still one of the rare countries where people eat a lot of uncooked fish, marinated in various ways or salted: something special for the visitor.

But the first Finnish fish to achieve international renown is the whitefish smoked whole. The bishops who came to pagan Finland long ago were given this special treat. In addition to whitefish, there is also an abundance of smoked rainbow trout. Smoking almost any kind of fish is the angler's favorite means of preparing his catch.

Tuoresuolattu siika tai lohi
Fresh-salted whitefish or salmon

For each kg of fish:
2 tbsp rock salt
1/4—1/2 tbsp sugar
1 tsp coarsely ground white pepper
dill fronds and stems

1. Clean and fillet the fish, but do not skin.
2. Place one of the fillets skin-side down in a dish and sprinkle with a mixture of salt, sugar, and white pepper. Sprinkle with chopped dill.
3. Place another fillet skin-side up on the first fillet.
4. Sprinkle the rest of the salt mixture and dill on it. Cover with a weight.
5. Keep in a cold place for a day.
6. Scrape the spices off the surface and slice thinly.
7. Serve with boiled potatoes (preferably new potatoes) and chopped dill.

Salmon is the king of fishes. Slightly salted, smoked, grilled, fried salmon — or fish of the salmon family — is an essential part of a feast. Rainbow trout is reasonably priced and popular also for everyday meals. Fish is generally seasoned with dill.

Well Worth Fishing — and Eating

You'll see at least these fish in Finland, and you should try them, too:

Even the child knows the *perch* as he pulls it out of the lake for his mother's chowder. The perch is also delicious fried or grilled. The saying goes, "There's more fat in a perch's head than in a poor man's cupboard." The largest perch ever caught in Finland weighed 3.6 kg, even though most of the fish one catches with a hook and line are only a few inches long. The perch is a popular ingredient for fish pasty, *kalakukko*. This pasty looks like a small rye bread but is actually the world's most ingenious "lunch box." You can eat the rye-bread "box" as well as its contents, fish and pork.

Eel. The saying "slippery as an eel" probably came from the fisherman who had to take this squirmy creature out of a trawl. Smoked eel is delicious, especially served with scrambled eggs. The heaviest Finnish eel: 4.850 kg.

The *pike* lives off the coast of Finland and in nearly all its lakes. Caught with a hook and line, net, or trawl, it is sold in Finland and exported to other European countries. The pike tastes good fried or boiled, with egg sauce or as pike à la Homburg (baked pike with cheese). It's also a common ingredient in fish soup. The largest pike — which the Finns call the "bandit of the waters" — weighed 25.5 kg, but the best fish weighs a kilo or two.

The *pike perch* is caught in lakes and along the coast with a net, drum net, or trawl. This fine fish, whose eyes have sparked off many sayings ("eyes bulging like a pike perch's"), weighs 15 kg at its largest, but about a kilo is more normal. The pike perch is often served in restaurants à la Walewska, but in Finland you can order pike perch à la Mannerheim: boiled pike perch with melted butter and grated horseradish. The pike perch can also be simply boiled or broiled, and it's always just as good.

Sinappikastike
Mustard dressing

1/2 l salad oil
1 dl French mustard
1 dl prepared mustard
1 dl wine vinegar
100 g sugar
4 tbsp finely chopped dill
salt
freshly-ground black pepper

1. Mix the mustard, salt, sugar, black pepper, and a drop of wine vinegar. Beat well.
2. Add the oil as you would in making mayonnaise. Add wine vinegar a bit at a time between additions of oil.
3. Mix in the finely chopped dill. Parsley and chives can also be used.

This dressing is excellent as such with salted fish and salted fish salads. If you want to serve it with meat, reduce the amount of sugar to 50 g. The dressing can also be perked up with schnapps, brandy, or madeira.

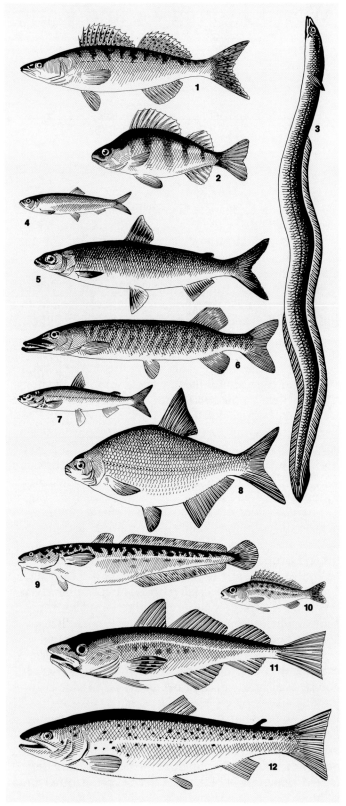

1. *Kuha* Pike perch *Lucioperca lucioperca*
2. *Ahven* Perch *Perca fluviatilis*
3. *Ankerias* Eel *Anguilla anguilla*
4. *Silakka* Baltic herring *Clupea harengus membras*
5. *Siika* Whitefish *Coregonus lavaretus*
6. *Hauki* Pike *Esox lucius*
7. *Muikku* Vendace *Coregonus albula*
8. *Lahna* Bream *Abramis brama*
9. *Made* Burbot *Lota lota*
10. *Kiiski* Ruffe *Acerina cernua*
11. *Turska* Cod *Gadus morhua*
12. *Lohi* Salmon *Salmo salar*

Kala paperissa
Fish in paper

bream, pike, whitefish, or any
other large fish
salt
baking paper
butter
newspaper

1. Clean the fish.
2. Rub inside and out with salt. Let the salt soak in for a couple of hours.
3. Dry with a paper towel.
4. Grease baking paper lightly with butter. Place the fish on the buttered area and roll into a tight package.
5. Wrap in several layers of newspaper.
6. Put the package onto coals in a bonfire or fireplace and let the paper burn slowly around the fish.
7. When the newspaper has burned down to the baking paper, the fish is done. This will take 15—25 minutes.
8. Peel off the paper and serve the fish hot or cold.

Potatoes are an essential part of Finnish food year round. New potatoes served with fresh dill, fish, or meat are one of the highlights of the summer months.

Uunilahna
Baked bream

a bream (c. 1 kg)
1 tbsp salt
c. 25 g butter or margarine

On top:
beaten egg
dried breadcrumbs
To baste:
cream, or water and cream

1. Clean, rinse, and dry the fish.
2. Rub with salt, inside and out.
3. Place the fish on a greased oven pan.
4. Brush the fish with beaten egg and sprinkle with dried breadcrumbs. Put the rest of the butter on top of the fish in dabs.
5. Bake in a hot oven, starting at 250°C. When the fish has browned, reduce the heat to 200°C. Baste with the fat from the pan.
6. Add some cream to the pan and let it boil.
7. Serve with boiled potatoes and a good salad.

The *bream* may be flat, and not terribly pretty, but it has delicious white meat. It's best in the spring and beginning of summer. The expression "lie around like a bream" refers to the way this fish lazes about in shallow waters. The largest bream weighed 11.5 kg. On weekends, men can be found huddled around smoking ovens breaking alder branches: smoking with alder suits the bream best.

The visitor sometimes has to unwrap this tasty fish from a thick envelope of paper, a handy way of baking fish. Bream can also be filled and baked in an oven in a more traditional way or cooked and served cold in aspic. A bream normally weighs around a kilo.

The cleaned fish is nailed on a board and cooked in the glow of a fire — a traditional fish from the West coast.

Ristiinnaulittu siika tai lohi
Nailed whitefish or salmon

a whitefish or salmon (c. 2 kg)
c. 1 tbsp of salt/kg of fish

1. Clean the fish and split it beside the backbone so that it can be opened easily.
2. Sprinkle with salt and keep in a cold place for a couple of hours.
3. Spread out the fish, skin-side down, on a wooden board with a long handle. Nail it on with clean wooden pegs or metal nails.
4. Broil the fish by a bonfire without the fire actually touching the fish. The process is slow and should take about an hour.
5. When the fish is brown and done, take it off the board.
6. Serve with melted butter or mushroom sauce and boiled potatoes.

The *salmon* is usually pulled out of the ocean or the rivers of Lapland. It is the most expensive and sought-after fish delicacy. "Red as a salmon," say the ordinary folk, who like their salmon pink. Try salted raw, boiled, grilled, in chowder. Any way! "When there's salmon, you don't need fish!" Grilled salmon fins: just a snack, but delicious. A more substantial meal is salmon pasty, *kulibiaka:* salmon, rice, eggs, and chopped dill in a pastry shell. The largest ocean salmon of all times weighed 43 kg.

The rainbow trout, from the unpolluted sea or lakes, has become an excellent and inexpensive fish for everyday meals. It is used the same way as salmon. Roe from the rainbow trout has become an important export item. This "red caviar" is available smoked or plain and is also called "the caviar of presidents."

Smoking fish or meat in the yard is a summer treat. Perch, bream, flounder, whitefish, and pike are smoked in homemade smoking barrels or special smoking boxes.

Fish soup is often prepared with milk. During the burbot season meals may start with roe sandwiches, followed by soup.

The *burbot* is a winter fish excellent for creaming or chowders. Its roe is a great delicacy, served with toast or *blinies,* buckwheat pancakes. "Pig's tongue and burbot liver are in a class with butter," goes the saying. The largest burbot weighed 10.5 kg, but at its best the burbot weighs 1 1/2 to 2 kg.

The *vendace* is an important lake fish, caught with a trap or net. Vendace roe is another delicacy. In a way, the vendace is Finland's sardine, usually the same size, although the largest vendace weighed just under a kilo. The saying goes of these large vendace, "If you eat one, it's not enough, but if you eat two, it's too much." The small "needle vendace," thumb's length, are good salted, washed down with schnapps.

If you're in luck, you'll be able to go on a lake excursion to eastern Finland and taste "fish cooked on the lake shore." This dish is made by cooking fatty vendace, water, onions, and lots of butter in a large pot. The aroma of the fish adds to the joy of eating outdoors, looking at the fire, and smelling the fragrant smoke.

The meat of the *turbot* is white and delicious. It's caught with a net along the shores of the Gulfs of Bothnia and Finland. In the summer you can buy it smoked, direct from the fishermen in the Åland Islands. Good! The largest turbot weighed 5 kg.

The *whitefish,* a relative of the salmon, is fatty, with fine meat. Smoked and cold on a buffet, marinated, fried, grilled, in a soup, or "nailed out," as a main dish, the whitefish is always delicious and so is its roe. It is caught with nets in the sea and in lakes. The largest whitefish topped the scales at 12 kg, though most weigh less than a kilo.

Madekeitto
Burbot soup

1 burbot, c. 1 kg
6 potatoes
2 onions
1/4 tsp whole allspice
salt
1/2 l water or fish broth
1/2 l milk
2 dl heavy cream or 1 dl sour cream
2 tbsp flour
dill

1. Peel and slice the potatoes. Dice the onions.
2. Put the vegetables in boiling water. Add salt and allspice. Cook for 10 minutes.

3. Add the fish, cut into serving pieces. Don't forget the delicious liver! Cook for 5 minutes.
4. Whisk the flour into the milk and add to the soup. Simmer for another 5 minutes.
5. Check to see that the soup is well seasoned. Add the cream or sour cream and sprinkle with chopped dill.

The soup can be made with different fish, for example salmon, whitefish, pike, perch, vendance, even Baltic herring.

The *Baltic herring* is Finland's most important fish, since it is available the year round, though spring and fall are its most important seasons. The silver flanked Baltic herring, 10—15 cm long, is delicious in both everyday dishes and specialties.

The Finns say that they never get tired of Baltic herring, and no wonder: there are so many recipes for this popular fish that they can fill a whole cookbook, and in fact do!

How is Baltic herring best? Everyone has his own favorite dish. Salted and smoked Baltic herring (the silver skin turns golden when smoked!) are popular, and so are fried and marinated Baltic herring. In fact, the fish can be made into imaginative casseroles and salads, served as fillets either flat or stuffed.

New dishes are Baltic herring tartare and herrings with garlic and mustard dressing. Industry has recognized the Baltic herring's potential and has started to pickle it in a sweet marinade like its big herring cousins from the north Atlantic. You can do what you like with the Baltic herring, but some Finns say you must eat it whole, head and all — that's the healthiest way.

The Finns are eating more and more fish these days. Fish is easy to prepare, especially when so many varieties are available already cleaned and filleted.

Rapusilakat
"Crayfish" herrings

600 g Baltic herring fillets
salt, black pepper
a bunch of dill with stalks
c. 2 1/2 dl tomato juice or
the same amount of crushed canned
tomatoes
butter

1. Grease a flame-proof casserole, saucepan, or frying pan.
2. Place the fillets, skin-side up, on a chopping board.
3. Sprinkle the fillets with salt, black pepper, and chopped dill.
4. Roll the fillets and place them side by side in the casserole or pan. Sprinkle with dill stalks and salt, and cover with tomato juice or crushed tomatoes.
5. Cover and simmer gently for c. 15 minutes.
6. Serve cold.

Paistetut silakat etikkaliemessä
Pickled Baltic herrings

1 kg Baltic herrings
salt
1—2 red onions, cut in rings
a bunch of dill, chopped finely
dark syrup

Marinade:
1 dl white vinegar
1 1/2 dl sugar
2 1/2 dl water
5 whole white peppercorns
5 whole cloves, crushed
Breading:
dried bread crumbs, salt
For frying:
butter or margarine

1. Clean the Baltic herrings, but do not remove the backbones. Rinse and drain well.
2. Salt the herrings lightly on the inside and press them back into shape.
3. Boil the marinade ingredients in a pot for 5 minutes. Strain and cool.
4. Salt the dried breadcrumbs lightly and bread the fish.
5. Fry over an even heat until golden brown on both sides.
6. Make alternate layers of herrings, onion rings, and chopped dill in a pretty jug or dish, dripping a bit of syrup between each layer.
7. Keep in a cool place until ready to serve.

Summertime — and the Night is White

In the summertime — June, July, August — the hay is fragrant, the red wild strawberries stand out along the roadsides, and night never comes.

Some say that the Finns are really only alive in summer. Finns have a summer expression, a summer feeling, summer habits, and summer foods. Finns also have a summer place, a cottage, and in summer, especially in July, it seems as if the whole of Finland is closed. Everyone's celebrating summer.

Summer is *Midsummer,* the traditional June festival, the nightless night when bonfires on the shores are reflected on the lakes — unless a forest fire warning has been issued.

In the province of Häme, people make pancakes. In Ostrobothnia, the traditional Midsummer weekend food is a kind of soup that has been cooked so long that the cheese in it turns red.

The first *new potatoes,* in June, are always a wonderful experience for the Finns. These tiny, finger-tip-sized, boiled new potatoes, *dill* from your own patch, and fresh butter. You don't need anything else. If you want a real feast, buy or make some fresh-salted salmon. But even ordinary herring is fine with new potatoes: it's fresh, too, brought by the Finnish fishing fleet from Icelandic waters.

For some people, the highlight of summer comes with the crayfish. The season starts on the 21st of July and ends in about the middle of September.

Summer means berries, too, but before the berries ripen, there is always rhubarb, for pies, puddings, and juice. Ice cream is a popular partner for rhubarb and for just about any other dessert. Enormous quantities of ice cream are devoured by the Finns in summer, and when the strawberries come, there's nothing better than vanilla ice cream and fresh strawberries.

The best place to buy juicy strawberries is at the market place. They're expensive at first, but who cares? At least one carton at the beginning of summer is a must. Later on, the cultivated strawberry is joined by wild strawberries and blueberries from the forests, and black and red currants from one's own bushes. Then there are cloudberries, raspberries, lingonberries, and cranberries.

Mesimarja, arctic bramble, Rubus arcticus

Vadelma, raspberry, Rubus idaeus

Pihlajanmarja, rowanberry, Sorbus aucuparia

Karpalo,
cranberry,
Vaccinium oxycoccus

Lakka, cloudberry, Rubus chamaemorus

Ahomansikka, wild strawberry, Fragaria vesca

Tyrnimarja, sea buckthorn, Hippophaë rhamnoides

Mustikka, blueberry, Vaccinium myrtillus

Puolukka,
lingonberry,
Vaccinium vitis-idaea

Summer food is simple, natural, and fresh. Water from a country well or spring is a joy, gulp by gulp, especially when you're used to chemical-filled city water. Tea tastes different and coffee is much better than in town. Fresh water is the best refresher as such or as a mixer.

Summer is a time for making birch sauna switches for winter use. They're dried or frozen so that the fragrance of the green leaves stays with them even in the electric saunas so common in apartment buildings.

Summer is sun, the deep blue sky, a sea of dandelions, life on the shores, and a lazy bicycle excursion.

It's taking the milk pail to the neighbor's barn, patting a horse in the corral, fetching the day-old newspaper from the village. It's chopping wood and collecting pine cones, clearing away branches, and repairing the dock.

It's taking a rod or net and fishing — then the inevitable work of untangling the net and cleaning the fish — and cooking fish delicacies any way you like.

It's a sizzling barbecue and the appetizing fragrance of pork ribs, steaks, or sausage, downed with a glass of cold beer.

Central Finland is a boater's delight. You can sit in a canoe or sail on a small, high, white-sided inland lake cruiser, its steam whistle echoing in the forests. Almost every family has a rowboat, and blisters are on everyone's hands. Some thoughtless intruders bother those used to peaceful lakes with their outboard motors and transistor radios.

There are sailboats on the larger bodies of water. Fishermen's motors putter. Vacationers enjoy themselves in the archipelagoes of the Gulfs of Finland and Bothnia.

You can pick an armful of wild flowers and laze around in a big farmhouse kitchen. Your nose will meet with the unmistakable fragrance of freshly baked blueberry pie.

Later on in the evening, you'll perhaps have a cup of *viili,* clabbered milk that is rather like elastic yogurt. Many people eat it at least once a day in summer. "You need nothing except a few sandwiches and maybe berries." The culture for making *viili* comes from a neighbor, the same neighbor who supplies the fresh milk. And the next day, there's a thick skim of cream on the top of the earthenware or glass cup above the sour, refreshing *viili.* It's

Mustikkakeitto
Blueberry soup

1 l water
1/2 l blueberries
1 1/2 dl sugar
2 tbsp potato flour

1. Put the water, blueberries, and sugar in a saucepan. Blend and cook for about five minutes.
2. Dissolve the potato flour in c. 1/2 dl water. Remove the boiling blueberry mixture from the stove. Add the potato flour liquid to the blueberry mixture, stirring well.
3. Put the saucepan back on the stove and bring to a boil. Remove from the heat as soon as the first bubbles appear.
4. Sprinkle with sugar and cool.
5. Serve cold with sweet rusks or cookies.

Home-baked crusty blueberry pie can also be filled with other berries or rhubarb.

Mustikkapiirakka
Blueberry pie

Crust;
150 g butter or margarine
(1/2 dl sugar)
1 egg
1/2 dl cream
2 1/2 dl flour
Filling:
c. 1 l blueberries
sugar
1 tbsp dried breadcrumbs or potato flour

1. Whisk the butter or margarine and add sugar, if desired.
2. Add the egg, mixing well, then the cream and flour in turns. Don't beat too much or the dough will get tough.
3. Let the dough stand for a while in a cool place.
4. Roll out the dough into a thin sheet on a baking pan.
5. Mix the blueberries with sugar and dried breadcrumbs or potato flour.
6. Spread the filling onto the dough and raise the edges.
7. Bake at 200°C until the crust is golden brown, c. 30 minutes.

25

eaten as such or perked up with sugar and ginger or cinnamon. *Talkkuna* (a mixture of powdered oats, barley, and peas) blended with *viili* makes a thick, delicious dish. It's not very attractive-looking — a bit gray and strange — but in spite of its primitive appearance, it's very nourishing. *Viili* and buttermilk can also be bought at the store in cartons of different sizes, and yogurts in a wide range of flavors are also available.

Another summer delight is *apposet,* pea pods, which are cooked as such, dipped in butter, and pulled through the teeth to remove the thin skins. People rush to make the summer's first produce into summer soup: milk and tender vegetables.

Kesäkeitto
Summer soup

1 l water
1/2 tbsp salt
2 medium-sized carrots
a small cauliflower
1—2 dl peas
2 dl young pea pods
1/4 l new potatoes
a few fresh spinach leaves
1—2 tbsp flour
1/2 l milk
butter
1 tsp sugar

On top:
finely chopped parsley

1. Heat the water and add salt.
2. Slice and add the carrots, and cook for about 5 minutes.
3. Dice the cauliflower and potatoes and add them to the soup with the peas and pea pods.
4. When the vegetables are almost done, add the milk and flour and then the spinach.
5. Simmer until all the ingredients are done.
6. Add a dab of butter and sprinkle with parsley.
7. Serve with dark bread or crispbread.

Raparperijuoma
Rhubarb drink

1 kg rhubarb
1 lemon
3/4 kg sugar
3 tbsp citric acid
2 1/2 l water

1. Cut the rhubarb into pieces. Wash the lemon thoroughly (use an unsprayed lemon if you can!) and cut into thin slices. Put the rhubarb, lemon, sugar, and citric acid into a large pot.
2. Bring the water to a boil and pour it over the other ingredients. Mix well to dissolve all the sugar.
3. Store the mixture in a cool place for a day. Sieve and bottle.
4. Serve ice cold, diluted with water.

Raparperihillo
Rhubarb jam

2 kg rhubarb
800 g sugar
2 lemons, sliced
boiling water

1. Peel and wash the rhubarb. Put it in a large bowl and add the sugar and lemon slices.
2. Pour over just enough boiling water to cover the ingredients well. Mix to dilute all the sugar. Cover and let stand for a day.
3. Sieve and bottle the syrup. Keep it in a cool place and dilute to serve.
4. Discard the lemon slices, but put the rhubarb into a saucepan and simmer it down to jam consistency. Bottle the jam and use it to fill a cake or as a topping for pancakes.

Pihlajanmarjajäädyke
Festive rowanberry parfait

2 egg yolks
2 1/2 dl confectioner's sugar
5 dl whipping cream
2—3 dl rowanberry purée
(3 tbsp rowanberry liqueur)

Topping:
whipped cream and whole rowanberries

1. Whisk together the egg yolks and sugar.
2. Whip the cream in a large bowl. Carefully fold in the yolk mixture, rowanberry purée, and liqueur, if used. Check to see that the mixture has a strong enough berry flavor.
3. Turn the mixture into a tube cake pan rinsed with water and freeze.
4. Dip the pan in hot water for a few seconds and turn the parfait onto a serving platter. Decorate with whipped cream and rowanberries.

Pakastettu pihlajanmarjahilloke
Rowanberry purée

1 l rowanberries
1 dl sugar
water

1. Cook the rowanberries in a small amount of water until they can be mashed or blended.
2. Add sugar.
3. Place in small containers and freeze.

The Night of the Crayfish

Keitetyt ravut
Boiled crayfish

40 medium-sized live crayfish
4 1/2 l water
1 1/2 dl rock salt
1—2 sugar cubes
dill crowns
dill fronds

1. Heat the water to boiling and add salt and sugar.
2. Make sure that all the crayfish are alive before you put them, head first, into the boiling water. Keep the water boiling as you add each crayfish. Cover with plenty of dill crowns.
3. When all the crayfish have been added, cook for 10 minutes. When the shell separates from the tail, the crayfish are ready.
4. Remove the dill from the pot. Put in new dill and cool the crayfish in the water.
5. Serve cold, with toast and butter, chopped dill, white wine, or beer and schnapps.

At the end of July, or at the beginning of August at the latest, the Finns begin to have crayfish parties. The official "opening night" is the 21st of July, when crayfish enthusiasts are allowed to catch any crayfish over 10 cm long.

Crayfish are eaten at dusk. The summer evening is the best backdrop for the long table, plates, bright red napkins, a bib for each diner, crayfish knives, a frosty bottle of schnapps, beer, toast, and piles of dill crowns and fronds — nearly everything you need for a traditional crayfish party.

The guests of honor at this feast are the crayfish. There's a great pot of them, 8 to 16 per person. Some people search among the red creatures to find the wide-hipped girl crayfish, which they consider best. Others covet the large, meaty claws. The main thing is that you can pick up the crayfish and eat it with your hands, suck the juice from the shell — it tastes like dill, which is used to season the cooking water. A cold shot of schnapps is drunk in honor of the tail, washed down with beer or mineral water. Tail meat is piled on toast, sprinkled with dill, and gobbled down in larger quantities at a time than would be polite on any other occasion.

Hunters start to clean their guns, first to shoot pigeon, later wild duck.

At this stage, people begin to predict what kind of mushroom season the fall will bring. The first — and to many the best — mushrooms, the chantarelles, have already raised their heads.

The 21st of July is a happy day for shellfish lovers — the day of the first crayfish catch. They are seasoned with dill, and served with beer, schnapps, white wine, or spring water.

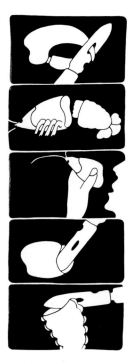

This is how to eat crayfish:

1. Suck the broth from the underside of the crayfish before opening.

2. Remove the claws, breaking the ends off and sucking out the juice. Remove the jointed part. Open the widest part of the claw with a crayfish knife to get the meat out. Suck all parts thoroughly.

3. Remove the tail from the shell. Drink the juice from the shell as you would from a glass.

4. Twist the shell from the "body." The bitter stomach usually comes out with it. Scrape the "crayfish butter" from the inside of the shell with a knife. Suck the middle of the crayfish and any roe with it.

5. Open the tail with a crayfish knife and dig out the meat. Remove the dark intestine from the center before eating.

Autumn Leaves and Mushrooms

The autumn — September, October, November — is a season of harvests and mushrooms.

The forests are filled with mushrooms and people looking for them. People are on the move for other reasons, too. The autumn is an active season. It brings the Finn back to work and his hobbies after the long summer rest. Social contacts start up again, people meet and talk.

Weekends far into the fall are still spent in the summer cottages. Yards have to be put into shape, leaves raked up, boats put into dry dock, saunas closed. And as we said, you just have to go on a mushroom hunt.

Most go mushroom hunting straight from their doorstep. Rubber boots on their feet, a basket on their arm, and a mushroom chart in their jacket pocket. A mushroom excursion is a chance to get a lot of fresh air and exercise, apples in the cheeks, a look at the lovely landscape, and above all mushrooms.

Forests would be just as profitable for mushrooms as they are for trees if only all of the edible mushrooms were used. A lot are left unpicked. There are about 500 edible varieties of mushrooms, about 30 of which are really worth eating. All in all, there are only a few truly poisonous mushrooms to beware of among the 2000 types that grow. And so one really does need an expert mushroom guide when going mushroom hunting.

After coming back from a mushroom hunt, you sort the mushrooms according to type and clean them. Some people rush right into the kitchen to heat up the frying pan. Mushrooms can be preserved and frozen, put in sauces, soups, and salads, and creamed.

Each mushroom has its own form and taste and personality, and that exciting foresty fragrance. Mushrooms are "vegetarian game," well worth hunting for! Take a look at just a few of the best on page *32—33*. Active mushroom enthusiasts have founded mushroom clubs in various parts of Finland. Commercial picking is also well organized.

The areas where mushrooms grow are vast. Mushroom picking is everyman's right. Here is a day's colorful catch of mushrooms.

Sienimuhennos
Creamed mushrooms

1 l good mushrooms (chantarelles, ceps, champignons, etc.) or 1/2—4 dl boiled or salted mushrooms
50 g butter or margarine
1 onion
4 tbsp flour
c. 1/2 l milk or milk and cream
salt, white and black pepper
(a bit of basil)

1. Clean the mushrooms. Boil if necessary. Dice the fresh mushrooms or chop the salted mushrooms finely.
2. Dice the onion.
3. Melt about half of the fat and add the mushrooms. Cook until the liquid evaporates.
4. Add the rest of the fat and the onion. Fry until the onion is transparent.
5. Sprinkle on the flour, and add the liquid little by little, stirring constantly.
6. Simmer under cover for 20 minutes. Add more liquid if necessary.
7. Season with salt and pepper, and basil, if you like.

To make mushroom soup, increase the amount of liquid and use bouillon for part of it.

The same recipe can be used with morels, but remember to cook fresh morels in plenty of water for ten minutes. Then discard the liquid and rinse the morels in cold water. If you use dried morels, you can use the water you soak them in since the poison disappears during the drying process. Morels should, however, be really dry, at least 4—5 months old.

Korvasieni,
morel,
Gyromitra esculenta.

Must be boiled before use.

Herkkutatti,
King mushroom or cep,
Boletus edulis

Suppilovahvero,
funnel-shaped chanterelle,
Cantharellus tubaeformis

Sienipikkelsi
Mushroom relish

1 1/2 dl small boiled chantarelles
or other small mushrooms

Liquid:
2 dl white vinegar
4 dl water
3 dl sugar
1 tsp salt
20 whole cloves
1/2 tsp whole allspice
1 bay leaf
a large piece of ginger

1. Put the boiled mushrooms into a jar.
2. Bring the rest of the ingredients to a boil and pour over the mushrooms.
3. Close the jar when the relish has cooled.
4. Serve as a condiment with meat or fish dishes or as a cocktail snack.

Musta torvisieni,
horn of plenty,
Craterellus cornucopioides

Haaparousku,
milky cap,
Lactarius trivialis

Kanttarelli,
yellow chanterelle,
Cantharellus cibarius

Sienisalaatti
Mushroom salad

1/2 l soaked salted mushrooms
1 small onion
2 dl sour cream or thick cream
ground black pepper or allspice
(lemon juice and a pinch or sugar)

1. Chop the soaked salted
mushrooms and onion very fine.
2. Whip the cream.
3. Mix the mushrooms with the
sour cream or whipped cream. (If
you like, season with lemon juice
and a pinch of sugar.)
4. Pour into a serving dish and
sprinkle with ground black pepper
or allspice.

Game hunting has very strict seasons. Pigeons, grouse, woodcocks, and ptarmigans are quite rare, but duck, snowgrouse, and hare are more easily available.

A Baltic herring fair is held in autumn: fishermen bring their boats up to the docks and sell lots of fish — fresh, smoked, pickled in barrels, salted. And perhaps also potatoes from the archipelago and sweet, black bread baked by the fishermen's wives back in the Åland Islands. People buy little barrels of pickled fish, Baltic herring rolls, and often sample them right out in the open, "from boat to mouth".

On the west coast, a delicacy eaten outdoors is the lamprey, that long eel-like creature which is also sold at this time of year in the rest of Finland. Lampreys are good grilled as such or dipped in mustard dressing, washed down with schnapps. They can also be bought pickled in vinegar.

This is the time when the vendace, whitefish, Baltic herring, and rainbow trout supply gourmets with *roe*.

The autumn starts the hunting season in earnest. For people in Finland, hunting at its best is a form of rest and relaxation, and not a real hunt for meat.

Lihakääryleet
Veal birds

1 kg roast of veal or moose or young beef
salt, white pepper

Filling:
c. 75 g butter
a bunch of parsley
Cooking broth:
c. 3 dl bouillon
1 dl thick cream
For frying:
butter

1. Cut small slices from the roast and pound them gently. Sprinkle with salt and white pepper.
2. Let the butter stand to soften and mix in the chopped parsley. Spread the mixture over the meat slices. Make small rolls and tie them with cotton thread or spear with a toothpick.
3. Brown the "birds" in butter. When all have been browned, add the bouillon and simmer over a low heat until tender.
4. Remove the thread or toothpicks. Arrange the rolls on a warmed platter.
5. Strain the broth, add cream, and boil for a few minutes. Pour over the rolls.
6. Serve, for example, with boiled potatoes, carrots, and pickled cucumbers.

You can hunt ringdoves, water fowl, pheasants, white ptarmigans, other forest birds, hares, moose, and white-tailed deer. You can also buy game, but not until September 16th. Certain forest birds and hares are never for sale.

White ptarmigan is hunted with and also with traps in the northernmost municipalities. The birds caught in traps are mostly sold by the Lapps.

Finnish hunters obey strict rules and keep track of where, what, and when they hunt. To hunt a moose or deer, you always need a special license. Everyone who wants to hunt also has to take a shooting test.

The red-capped men on the edge of the fields in autumn are moose hunters, in case you wondered.

With good luck, you'll be able to sample some good game, though your host may play a trick or two on you. A strong, good soup was served to a guest one time. The guest loved it and had some more, but was upset when he heard the secret of its great taste: the bear that was its main ingredient!

Perhaps the best way to try game — including bear — is at a restaurant. There is a game sauce served with the meat, often a green salad and a special-tasting jam or jelly. Rowanberry, cranberry, and black currant jellies are especially good.

Moose hunters — often a hunting group — must obtain a license. The annual number of licenses alotted varies. Moose meat is generally prepared like beef and often served with other "game" from the forest, like berries and mushrooms, which here accompany the moose rolls. They are prepared in the same way as veal birds.

Winter Darkness — Christmas Lights

Blinit
Blinies

2 dl lukewarm water
25 g fresh yeast or 1/2 package dried yeast
1 dl cream
2 dl flour
3 dl buckwheat flour
c. 4 dl hot milk
c. 1 tsp salt
2 tbsp melted butter
2 eggs

1. Crumble the fresh yeast into lukewarm water or sprinkle on the dried yeast to dissolve it.
2. Add the cream and whip in the flours.
3. Let the batter stand, preferably for 12 hours or overnight.
4. Add hot milk, salt, melted butter, and egg yolks to the batter.
5. Whip the whites and fold them into the batter just before frying.
6. Fry on both sides in a special bliny or pancake pan, forming thick cakes.
7. Serve hot, straight from the pan.

When the first bit of ice starts to cover the water, it's time to catch that typical winter fish, the burbot. A skillful fellow will hit the burbot over the head through the thin ice just offshore. The burbot has the finest roe, which is served with *blinies,* sour cream, and raw onions.

The Finns can create quite a debate or parlor game around red caviar or fish eggs: is fish roe just a poor substitute for caviar, or is it actually a delicacy all its own which it is useless to compare with caviar?

Caviar naturally has its partisans, but the patriotic Finn is always prepared to present, defend, praise, even extol Finnish roe.

What is roe?

The sturgeon doesn't swim around Finnish waters, but this land of over 60,000 lakes does have its own spawners. The cold climate makes fish spawn even in cold water, so there is plenty of excellent roe even in the dead of winter.

In fact, one of the most popular kinds of roe, from the burbot, has its peak season around Christmas.

If winter is the time for burbot roe, then autumn brings whitefish roe and roe from the little relative of the salmon, the vendace. Roe from the rainbow trout is available the year round. It can be bought lightly salted, but also delicately smoked, giving a more pungent taste. These are the "main roes". There are roe enthusiasts who are always ready to proclaim the finer points of roe from the pike, bullhead, Baltic herring, and smelt. But the burbot, whitefish, and vendace are fine with everyone.

Even though roe is expensive, it is not exorbitant. It is also possible to buy spawners — for example the burbot — and remove the roe yourself, which makes it much cheaper. Many Finnish anglers catch their own spawners.

How should roe be eaten? Why not try the classic Russian manner, with *blinies* — buckwheat pancakes — served with melted butter, sour cream, diced raw onions, and freshly ground black pepper. Many people mix burbot roe with whipped cream, cook and grind up the burbot liver to add to it, and season the delicacy with allspice.

Roe also tastes wonderful on toast — white or black. One school accepts roe only as an accompaniment to boiled or baked potatoes. And here's another question for debate: should the diced onion, roe, and sour cream be served separately, or may the hostess mix them together in a bowl?

Almost everyone agrees that a little glass of crystal-clear Finnish vodka accompanying any kind of roe served any way only enhances the roe enthusiast's pleasure.

Martinmas comes in November, and with it a fine goose dinner. The tradition is disappearing, but it's still possible to get goose preceded by "black soup," made from blood.

Finnish berry syrups are important not just to satisfy a thirst, but also as the best "cure" for a cold. Berry liqueurs have a taste of summer. The winter's favorite hot drink is *glögi* — hot spiced red wine or juice with almonds and raisins served at every Christmas party.

Christmas has always been a holiday when the Finns eat a lot. They admit that at Christmas they gorge themselves. They have a bad conscience, too, since every year they promise that next year they'll show a bit more restraint. But each Christmas every family serves as magnificent a Christmas meal as the purse can afford.

The Christmas meal begins with cold cuts: herring in different dressings and with different garnishes, slightly salted salmon, roe, smoked whitefish. Salads, sausages, in some families the traditional pasty and bouillon — and then the main dish, ham.

On the side are peas and prunes, that "must," rutabaga casserole, and often a potato casserole, liver casserole, and even carrot casserole. There are families which have traded the baked ham in for turkey, and others which don't have enough room for dessert — fruit salad, rice porridge, prune and cream pudding. In any case, the Christmas eating tradition is quite a heavy one. The family doesn't go anywhere for a few days after Christmas. At most they slice a few pieces off the Christmas ham and devour a few books. (Publishers bring out their best autumn books just in time for the holidays.)

Christmas meals also include fruit imported from the south, prunes, raisins, and ginger cookies, which

Ham is staple Christmas fare, though occasionally replaced by turkey or goose. Potato, rutabaga, liver, and carrot casseroles are also a must at Christmas time.

spread their fragrance throughout every home just before Christmas. Nutcrackers get a real workout, candles are burned, and the Christmas tree is just as bright and gaudy as it should be.

The fragrance of baking is an important part of life around Christmas. Just before the holidays, the traditional ginger cookies are made, which get better and better in the cookie jar. Closer to Christmas Day, it's time to make coffee bread, perhaps a few raisin cakes, and lots and lots of Christmas tarts.

They're pastry dough crescents or star-shaped creations filled with prune jam. Good with coffee and as a dessert even after Christmas.

Winter doesn't just bring snow, it also brings its opposite: darkness. It's good to be inside. The Finns have to spend a lot of money to build their homes, since they must line them inside and out to make them snug and warm. They sit by the fire, sleep, eat enough in between, and taste the delicacies they've put away as preserves.

Home-cooked food in winter is simple and warming: casseroles and soups, potatoes and gravies. Pea soup and oven pancakes are a good example. They're Shrove Tuesday food, actually, but good at other times of the year, too. The connoisseur warms up a glass of hot punch, Swedish style, to go with his soup. Not a bad combination.

The delicious Shrove Tuesday bun is a tradition. Some eat it as a dessert in hot milk. Others cut off its top like a hat and fill it with a bit of whipped cream before the hat is put on again. The bun can also be filled with almond paste. The fifth of February is Runeberg's Day, in honor of Finland's national poet. It's the season to eat Runeberg tarts, cupcakes which were first concocted from breadcrumbs, raspberry jam, and other ingredients by the thrifty Mrs. Runeberg.

Hot berry juice, tea, and hot chocolate are served in the evenings or after a skiing expedition. And when guests arrive, it's easy to warm up a bit of *glögi,* perhaps made with white wine this time. And as a snack, a winter delicacy, roe with blinies.

Joulukinkku
Christmas ham

a salted ham (4—5 kg)

On top:
1 egg yolk
2 tbsp mustard
1 tbsp sugar, preferably brown sugar
2 tbsp dried breadcrumbs

1. Dry the ham with a paper towel. Insert a meat thermometer at the thickest place, without touching the bone.
2. Bake at 160°C until the thermometer shows the right temperature for ham.
3. Remove the thermometer and increase the temperature to 225°C.
4. Skin the ham, leaving on the fat.
5. Blend the egg yolk and mustard, and spread over the fat.
6. Mix the sugar and breadcrumbs and sprinkle over the ham.
7. Return the ham to the oven and bake until the breadcrumbs are slightly browned.
8. Serve garnished with prunes, peas, cooked apple slices, accompanied by mustard and rutabaga casserole.

"Sillisalaatti" (herring salad) contains little cubes of cooked vegetables and tiny strips of herring or salted Baltic herring. Without the fish it's a vegetarian dish.

An almond in rice porridge is a good luck omen for the finder.

Lasimestarin silli
Glass master's herring

2 salt herrings
water
1 carrot
1 onion, preferably red
whole allspice
whole white peppercorns
whole cloves
1 bay leaf
(1 tbsp mustard seeds)

Liquid:
1 1/2 dl vinegar
2 dl water
1 1/2 dl sugar

1. Soak the herrings for a day, changing the water a couple of times.
2. Clean the herrings and cut off the skin on the underside. Cut into serving pieces.
3. Place the pieces in a glass jar in layers together with onion rings, carrot slices, and spices.
4. Bring the liquid ingredients to a boil, then let the mixture cool.
5. Pour the cold liquid over the herring slices.
6. Store in a cold place for a few days.
7. Serve with boiled potatoes.

Sillisalaatti
Herring salad

matjes herring fillets
2 beets
2 medium-sized carrots
2—3 potatoes
1 salted or dill pickle
1 apple
1 small onion
a dash of vinegar

On top:
hardboiled egg
Dressing:
sour cream or 1 dl whipping cream

1. Cook, peel, and dice the vegetables.
2. Mix the salad ingredients and place on a serving dish.
3. Soak a few pieces of beet in the vinegar to give it color.
4. Whip the cream and season it with a few drops of dyed vinegar, salt, pepper, and sugar.
5. Garnish with lettuce, but serve the hardboiled egg and dressing separately.

Imelletty perunalaatikko
Sweet-flavored potato casserole

1 kg potatoes
water
2 tbsp flour
2 tsp salt
c. 3 1/2 dl milk
1 tbsp butter

1. Boil the unpeeled potatoes, the peel and mash them.
2. While the mashed potatoes are still warm, mix in the flour. Cover the dish and let the mixture stand at room temperature for 3—4 hours.
3. Taste the mixture. If it is not sweet enough, add a little sugar. Add the salt, milk, and butter.
4. Grease an ovenproof casserole and pour in the mixture in it. Leave space for the casserole to rise.
5. Bake for 1—2 hours at 150 °C.

Lanttulaatikko
Rutabaga casserole

1 large rutabaga or 2 small ones
water, pinch of salt
1 dl cream
1/2 dl dried breadcrumbs
2 eggs
c. 1/2 dl syrup
a bit of grated nutmeg
rutabaga cooking broth

1. Cook the peeled, cubed rutabaga until soft in slightly salted water.
2. When the rutabaga is done, drain and mash or put through a blender.
3. Let the breadcrumbs swell in the cream and add to the rutabaga.
4. Beat the eggs and add together with syrup and nutmeg. Add a bit of cooking broth if the mixture is too thick.
5. Grease an oven-proof casserole and pour in the mixture. Pattern the top with a spoon. Bake at 175°C for about an hour.

Maksalaatikko
Liver casserole

2 dl raw rice or 1 1/2 dl barley groats
1/2 l water
c. 3 tsp salt
1 tbsp butter, margarine, or oil
1 small onion
300 g ground liver
1 dl syrup
1 tsp ginger
1 dl raisins
1 tsp marjoram
1/4 tsp white pepper
1/2 l milk
1 small egg
butter or margarine

1. Cook the rice or barley groats in the salted water.
2. Fry the diced onion in fat until transparent.
3. Mix all the ingredients into a thin batter, and pour into a greased, oven-proof casserole.
4. Top with a few dabs of butter.
5. Bake at 175°C for 45—60 minutes.
6. Serve with lingonberry jam or purée.

Vasikanpaisti
Old-fashioned roast veal

1 1/2 — 2 kg veal roast
2—3 onions, diced
2—3 carrots, diced
salt, white pepper
1—2 bay leaves
water

Gravy:
2 dl broth
1 tbsp flour
c. 1 dl thick cream

1. Rub the roast with salt and pepper. Place it in a shallow pan and top with a few pats of butter. Put the diced vegetables beside it.
2. Roast the meat in a 250°C oven for 1/2 hour. Reduce the temperature to 175°C and roast for another 1/2 hour *per kilo*. Baste during roasting. This old-fashioned roast veal should be well-done, but not dry.
3. Pour off the roasting juices. Thicken with flour and add the cream. Bring the gravy to a boil and season to taste.

Star-shaped, prune-filled tarts are served at Christmas time

Joulutortut
Christmas tarts

Pastry:
200 g soft butter or margarine
2 1/2 dl flour
1 dl cold water
1 tsp vinegar
Filling:
sweetened prune purée or plum jam

1. Put all the pastry ingredients into a bowl and mix quickly by hand into a dough. Don't knead too much.
2. Put the dough in a cold place to harden.
3. Roll out on a floured board, folding a few times to make a puff pastry, and finally make a sheet 1/2 cm thick.
4. Cut the sheet into 7 × 7 cm squares. Split the corners of each square.
5. Place a bit of prune purée or plum jam in the middle of each square. Fold over every other split end onto the center, to form a windmill-like tart.
6. Brush with beaten egg and bake at 250°C until light brown.

To make round tarts, cut into circles, fill, and fold in half. Bake as above. Both types of Christmas tart are popular in Finland.

Kaalilaatikko
Ground meat and cabbage stew

300 g ground meat (pork and beef mixture or lamb)
a medium-sized young cabbage
cooking oil
3 onions
3 summer carrots
water
1/8 tsp whole allspice
1—2 twigs of marjoram

1. Shred the cabbage. Dice the onions and carrots.
2. Heat a bit of oil and brown the meat. Add the onions, carrots, and cabbage. Mix and simmer a moment without any liquid.
3. Add the seasonings and a bit of water. You can also add a table-spoon of syrup. Cover and simmer gently for about an hour. A young cabbage cooks quickly, while an older one takes longer.
4. Serve with new potatoes. If you like tangy accompaniments, use puréed red currants or lingon-berries/cowberries to liven up the meal.

Lammaskaali
Baked mutton cabbage

1 kg mutton (shoulder, side, etc.)
2—3 kg cabbage
3 carrots
whole allspice
salt

For frying:
butter, margarine, or oil

1. Cut up the mutton and brown the pieces in hot fat on a frying pan.
2. Cut the cabbage into wedges and dice the peeled carrots.
3. Place the cabbage, meat, car-rots, and spices in layers in an oven-proof casserole.
4. Add a bit of water to the frying pan and pour the juice into the casserole.
5. Cover and simmer in a 200°C oven for 2 — 2 1/2 hours.
6. Serve with tomatoes or lingonberry purée.

Lohilaatikko
Salmon casserole

1 l peeled, sliced potatoes
c. 150 g salted salmon
2 tbsp chives and dill or
1 tbsp finely chopped onion
2 eggs
4 dl milk
a pinch of white pepper
1—2 tbsp dried breadcrumbs
a few dabs of butter

1. Grease an oven-proof casserole.
2. Cut the salted salmon into strips.
3. Place a layer of sliced potatoes on the bottom of the casserole and then a layer of salmon and chopped greens. Cover with another layer of potatoes.
4. Beat the eggs and add milk. Season with a pinch of white pepper.
5. Pour the mixture over the potatoes and salmon.
6. Sprinkle with dried bread-crumbs and top with a few dabs of butter.
7. Bake at 180°C for 45—60 minutes, until the potatoes are tender.

You can also make Baltic herring casserole this way, but top the fish with a layer of fat pork or bacon, add more fish and potatoes, and finish off with pork or bacon.

Lihakeitto
Vegetable beef soup

1 1/4 l water
1/2 tbsp salt
c. 1/2 kg beef with bones
1 small onion
1/4 tsp whole allspice
a piece of rutabaga
2 carrots
1 piece of celeriac
1 piece of parsnip
1 small leek
4 potatoes
parsley

1. Heat the salted water in a large kettle. When the water is lukewarm, add the meat.
2. Cook until foam forms on the surface. Skim.
3. Add the allspice, rutabaga, and diced carrots.
4. Cook until the meat starts to turn tender. Then add the diced celeriac and parsnip.
5. When the meat is tender, lift it onto a cutting board. Cut up the potatoes, slice the leek into rings, and add to the soup.
6. Separate the bones from the meat. Cut the meat into cubes and put back into the soup.
7. Season to taste.
8. Serve piping hot, garnished with parsley.

Hernekeitto
Pea soup

1 1/2 — 2 l water
4 dl dried peas
1/2 kg pig's trotters, part of it smoked, if available
salt
1 tsp marjoram
a bit of mustard

1. Rinse the peas and soak them overnight in cold water.
2. Cook the peas in the same water the next day.
3. Add the pork to the pot and simmer, covered, for about 3 hours.
4. When the meat is done, take it out of the pot; remove the skin and bone. Cut the meat into cubes and add to the soup.
5. Season and serve hot.

Siskonmakkarakeitto
Pork sausage soup

(serves 3—4)

1 l beef bouillon
big pieces of celery root, shredded
1 leek, sliced
1 carrot, slivered
5—5 potatoes, cubed
1/8 tsp whole allspice
8 or more fresh pork sausages
(1—2 dl sour cream)
parsley

1. Put the vegetables and allspice into the boiling bouillon. Simmer for about 10 minutes.
2. Slowly squeeze small amounts of the sausage from the casing direct into the soup. Cook for another 8 minutes.
3. If you use sour cream, mix it into the soup after it has boiled.
4. Season to taste. Garnish with parsley and serve with hardtack sandwiches.

Note:
Very soft pork sausages *(siskon-makkarat)* are used in Finland for this soup. If you use a firmer variety, cut into small pieces and cook as above, skinning or not, as necessary.

A cavalcade of seasonal and local specialties

5. | 8.

1. | 3.   6. | 9.

2. | 4.   7. | 10.

1. ''Mämmi'' — a sweet dish prepared with rye and malt, which are both cooked and baked.
2. Small pancakes with berry jams. Cold milk goes best with them.
3. Shrove Tuesdays buns — white buns served with almond paste, jam, or whipped cream.
4. ''Viili,'' cool clabbered milk, is a lovely summer dish, which Finns now enjoy year round.
5. Mignon egg — a real egg shell filled with the finest chocolate nougat.
6. ''Kalakukko'' — fish pasty — fish and fat pork baked inside a rye dough shell.
7. Small ''needle'' vendace — a treat from Kuusamo lakes — served either salted, baked, or as ''muikku fritti.''
8. ''Tippaleipä'' — a May Day cookie.
9. The ingredients of black sausage are blood, onions, and barley.
10. Lampreys — an autumn delicacy — are grilled and eaten with mustard sauce.

Where and What to Eat

There isn't a very long tradition of eating out in Finland, but today there are plenty of good places for dining out wherever you are. Your hotel has a restaurant, there are well-known, even famous gourmet restaurants, and intimate little bistros.

Some Finnish towns have restaurant guides in English, some of them with "reviews" of each place's menu.

Restaurants in Finland are classified according to the types of alcoholic beverages they are licensed to serve, from de luxe class international restaurants to the smallest beer joints.

The word *ravintola,* restaurant, always means a slightly more distinguished place for dining. One goes to a restaurant to entertain business associates, for dinner on Sundays, to commemorate a special event or family celebration, to dance or watch a floorshow. A *ravintola* has starched tablecloths and linen napkins.

Finnish restaurants serve international foods, those standard items whose names never change in any language. On the à la carte menu there are the usual steaks and cutlets, asparagus soup, omelets, parfaits, and ice cream.

Today Finnish menus are more international than ever before: fish in butter sauces, beef, pork, or veal noisettes in tempting sauces, rosy pink breast of duck, rainbow trout terrine, lamb stews, broilers in various forms, shellfish.

Restaurants naturally also serve what is called "Finnish food." Some of the most expensive dishes are often presented as typically Finnish: salmon or reindeer prepared in various ways. Real everyday Finnish food can't be had at all restaurants — things like pea or meat soup, Baltic herring casserole, cab-

Finland has a good choice of restaurants, from small cafés to luxury hotels. The cuisine is international — with a Finnish touch.

Lohitartar
Salmon steak tartare

(for 4)

400 g lightly salted salmon
1 tbsp dill
1 tbsp mayonnaise
1 tbsp sour cream or crème fraîche
1 tbsp cream
a few drops of lemon juice
(salt)
freshly ground white pepper

To decorate:
fish roe
Accompaniments:
toasted black or white bread

1. Dice the salmon into tiny cubes. Chop the dill finely.
2. Mix the ingredients in a bowl. Season with lemon juice, white pepper, and salt, if necessary. Check the seasonings.
3. Form the mixture into serving portions just as you would beef steak tartare.
4. Decorate with fish roe and sprigs of dill.
5. Serve with toast.

46

bage rolls, roast veal, meatballs, sausage, and pork gravies.

A few more words about the menu. In addition to à la carte dishes, there is also a lunch (served from 11 to 15.00) and dinner menu. This is always the most economical way to eat out, since the set menu includes an appetizer, entrée, dessert and/or coffee.

And what if it's not on the menu? You can always talk with the head waiter. The Finnish kitchen is able to produce on short notice such varied and completely realiable dishes as omelets, soups, and hot sandwiches.

Now back to everyday and home-made food. Rarely does the visitor realize that the word *baari* means a kind of restaurant. A *baari* is just less expensive than a restaurant and doesn't serve alcohol, or at most serves medium-strength beer. And this kind of "bar" doesn't always have a bar at all, with high stools and bartender. There are small tables, and it's all self-service. If you want bartenders, go to a bar in a larger restaurant or one of those homey, dim, smoky places in hotels with a clientele much the same as that of any bar, regardless of the time of night or day.

A food bar, *ruokabaari,* has the fastest service for coffee, tea, refreshments, cold sandwiches, and rolls. But some bars also know how to make real home-cooked meals: the typical meatball served in brown gravy, garnished with pickles, beets, and tomatoes, and served with potatoes. It's also possible to get a good bowl of meat and potato soup, or liver casserole. And there's porridge at any time of day, that dish of soft, hot oatmeal or other grain served with a dab of butter in the middle.

Some types of *baari* confuse the issue even more and use the words *kahvila-café.* There are unfortunately only a few real Viennese-style cafés. Today's café is an efficient place. There's no time to linger elegantly over a newspaper, hot chocolate, and a pastry. No, cafés serve assembly-line meals warmed in microwave ovens, pizzas, salads, hamburgers, for those working in offices and stores in the center of town who must rush out and grab a bit to eat on their lunch hour.

And how about the *grilli?* A grill may be joined to a restaurant or a bar and serves quickly-prepared grilled foods, especially meat. There are grills licensed to serve wine or beer, but some hole-in-the-wall grills only serve sausages, pasties, hamburgers, milk, and soft drinks.

Paistetut ahvenet à la Havis Amanda
Spawner perch à la Havis Amanda

2—4 perch fillets per person
soft white breadcrumbs
hardboiled eggs
perch roe
chopped dill
butter
salt, black pepper

1. First prepare the ingredients for the sauce. Dice the yolks and whites separately. Remove the roe from the sacs and put in a separate dish.
2. Bread the fillets and fry quickly on both sides. Season with salt and pepper. Remove from the pan and keep hot.
3. To make the sauce, melt the butter on the pan. Add the boiled diced egg yolks and whites, roe, and dill. Heat quickly and season to taste.
4. Pour the sauce over the fillets and serve immediately.

Sillijäätelö
Herring ice cream

(for 6)

6 pickled herring or matjes herring fillets, with their marinade
1 onion
freshly ground white pepper
chives
4 dl whipping cream

1. Cut the herrings into small pieces.
2. Dice the onion.
3. Whip the cream and mix in the herring pieces and diced onion. Then carefully fold in a bit of marinade to give the mixture color.
4. Season with pepper and chopped chives.
5. Pour into a suitable dish and freeze.
6. Serve as a first course with boiled potatoes.

To vary, use anchovies instead of herring. Use dill instead of chives.

There's also a kind of "speedy grill" — the hot-dog stand, or *nakkikioski*. In addition to hot dogs, there are various kinds of pasties and Finnish-type hamburgers, where the meat patty is replaced by a slice of sausage, topped with catsup, mustard, onion, relish. The *nakki* is a long, skinny, good-tasting hot-dog. Many people stop by these lighted stands at night because the mustard is strong and doesn't taste store-bought.

Service in Finnish restaurants is somewhat slower than on the Continent and waiters don't always have a wide range of languages at their command. Happily, the menu is often also printed in English, German, and French.

There's plenty of admirable enterprise in Finnish restaurants. It's a shame that an unjustified modesty evidently prevents them from bringing to light the specialties of their "own" Finnish cuisine.

The restaurant-goer should not be startled if the lights go out in the middle of the evening. That means that no more orders will be taken. The lights are generally flashed on and off 30—45 minutes before the restaurant closes. A conscientious waitress always remembers to ask in time, "Anything else before the lights go out?"

Roe is here served in aspic, with a neat roll of salmon on top.

Riimihärkää Mäkelän tapaan
Cured fillet of beef à la Mäkelä

500 g fillet of beef, cut from the
center
50 g coarse salt
25 g sugar
10 whole white peppercorns
10 whole black peppercorns
8 cl madeira

1. Crush the peppercorns roughly
and mix with the salt and sugar.
2. Carefully remove all fat and
muscle sheath from the fillet. Roll
the fillet in the mixture, pressing it
down gently.
3. Pour the madeira into a stainless
steel, enamel, or porcelain dish
and add the fillet.
4. Refrigerate the meat for 3 days,
turning it daily.
5. Wrap the meat tightly in plastic
wrap and refrigerate it for 4 more
days.
6. Freeze the meat before cutting
it either by machine or with a
sharp knife into the thinnest possible slices.
7. Serve, for example, with
mustard dressing.

Silakkapihvit
Baltic herring fillets

1 kg Baltic herrings
salt, white pepper
dill, chives

To bread:
rye flour, salt
To fry:
butter or margarine

1. Clean and rinse the fish and
remove head and spine.
2. Place half of the fillets skin-
side down.
3. Sprinkle with salt and white
pepper and a layer of chopped dill
and chives. Top with an unseasoned
fillet.
4. Turn the paired fillets in rye
flour and salt.
5. Fry until golden brown.
6. If you want to serve the fish
with a sauce, add cream to the
pan after frying. When it boils,
it's ready.

Täytetty hauki
Stuffed pike

a pike (1 — 1 1/2 kg)
c. 1 1/2 tsp salt

Stuffing:
1 dl raw rice
2 hardboiled eggs
cream
salt, white pepper
On top:
melted butter
dried breadcrumbs

1. Scale and clean the fish. Leave
the head on.
2. Rub the fish, inside and out,
with salt. Let the salt soak in for
an hour or so.
3. Cook the rice in salted water.
Drain if necessary.
4. Dice the hardboiled eggs and
add the rice and a bit of cream.
Season to taste.
5. Place the pike on a greased
oven-proof dish and stuff with the
rice and egg mixture.
6. Brush the fish on both sides
with melted butter and sprinkle
with breadcrumbs.
7. Bake in a 225°C oven until the
fish is slightly browned. Reduce
the temperature to 180—200°C.
Add a bit of water and cream to
the pan. Baste the fish with the
mixture occasionally.
8. When the fish is golden brown
and the fins are loose when pulled,
the pike is done. This will take
30—40 minutes, depending on the
size of the fish.

Paistetut lohileikkeet
Fried salmon steaks

a thick salmon steak per person
butter
salt, white pepper
dill

1. Fry the salmon *just before serv-*
ing: melt the butter on the pan
and fry the salmon steaks on a
low heat until just done — no
longer! Season with salt and pepper.
2. Place on a serving platter and
decorate with chopped dill.
3. Serve with fried mushrooms
and patty shells with a filling of
Jerusalem artichokes and celery.

Lohipiirakka
Kulibiaka — salmon and rice pasty

Crust:
3 dl flour
200 g butter or margarine
c. 1 dl cold water
Filling:
3 dl cooked rice
2 hardboiled eggs
a bunch of fresh dill
1 can of salmon or 300 g fresh or
slightly salted salmon
salt, white or black pepper

1. To make the crust, cut the butter or margarine into the flour
with two knives, a pastry blender,
or your fingertips. When the mixture is granular, add the water and
toss quickly into a dough.
2. Let the dough stand for a while
in a cold place.
3. Roll out the dough on a floured
baking table into a rectangular
sheet c. 1/2 cm thick.
4. Place half of the rice in the
center of the sheet, then add layers
of sliced egg, salmon, dill, seasonings, and the rest of the rice.
5. Lift the edges of the crust over
the filling and press them together
with a fork or your fingers.
6. Brush the crust with beaten egg
and prick with a fork.
7. Bake in a 200°C oven until
golden brown, about 30 minutes.
8. Serve warm plain or with
melted butter seasoned with dill.

The Smörgåsbord, "voileipäpöytä," is a Finnish Banquet

When he hears the word *smörgåsbord,* the Finn says, or at least thinks, "Lead us not into temptation..." Then he walks around the buffet table and picks and chooses, piles the food up, spoons it on, searches, gleans...

The smörgåsbord is a self-service affair, but older than the supermarket. It's a way to rationalize, let the individual have a chance to choose as he likes, measure his own endurance in front of an abundance of temptations.

When the Finns in days gone by had great banquets, a special buffet was filled with food for the guests. The banquets lasted two days, sometimes as long as a week. Banquets were held on major holidays, at weddings and funerals.

Preparations were made well in advance. The cooks arrived a week or so ahead of time. A calf was slaughtered, perhaps a sheep, too. The cooks did their best: their honor and the honor of the house was at stake.

Dining was the highlight of the banquet.

To begin with there was the buffet, which might have

> — a salad; head cheese; salted bream or
> whitefish; herring; cold steamed fish; smoked
> meat; home-made cheese; rutabaga, potato,
> and liver casseroles; various types of bread.

After the guests had had their fill of the buffet, there was a between-course snack: bouillon and puff pasties or fruit soup made with raisins or mixed fruit, garnished with whipped cream.

The main courses might be

> — roast meat; gravy; boiled
> potatoes; lingonberry purée.

And for dessert there was

> — rice porridge or prune fool, perhaps layer
> cakes and pastries.

The beverage was home-made beer.

This tradition is what gave birth to the modern-day Finnish smörgåsbord, which has changed enormously over the decades. A smörgåsbord is a rare phenomenon: when a restaurant sets one up, it's an

51

occasion. Some restaurants always have a cold buffet, while others have one once a week.

The buffets on the ships that sail between Finland and Sweden and between Finland and the Federal Republic of Germany give a good idea of what the Finns want in a buffet these days.

There are no two identical smörgåsbord tables. That's one of its fascinations. Around the world, from New York to the Canary Islands, the smörgåsbord is known as a Scandinavian specialty. The Finn, of course, thinks that the Finnish smörgåsbord is the finest of its kind, the "real" one, the most bountiful, the tastiest.

The basic ingredients for the smörgåsbord come from the sea, the lakes, forests, and fields. In addition to a sturdy basis, fish and meat, there should also be plenty of condiments, salads, and snacks. Bread, butter, and cheese are included, too, of course.

The table isn't set any which way. It's well thought out and lovely; it has to be, in order to be appetizing. The tablecloth, dishes, cutlery, and flowers all form an entity.

The first phase is the most important, at least that's what fish and herring lovers say. You see, you should always start with the fish. There's plenty to choose from and the waitress changes plates between courses. You'll find:

    — Russian herring; Glass master's herring; salted vendace; Baltic herring rolls; cobbler's salmon; smoked Baltic herring; fresh-salted Baltic salmon; grilled lamprey; boiled salmon fin; smoked whitefish; roe (vendace, whitefish, or burbot); anchovies; shrimp; smoked eel; bream; pike perch, or rainbow trout in aspic; sardines; mackerel.

With the fish, there are hot potatoes — and preferably a glass of clear, cold schnapps. After the fish, there's meat, usually at the end of the table on the upper "shelf."

For example, there's

    — ham; various kinds of sliced sausage; roast beef; reindeer tongue; smoked mutton; head cheese; pâté; cold little meatballs; roast veal; pig's trotters; tongue.

Some restaurants are proud of their fowl, for example:

    — turkey; pheasant; chicken; ptarmigan; wild duck.

You can lighten up the meal a bit with:

The Finnish "voileipäpöytä" or "pitopöytä" (smörgåsbord) is prepared whenever a large group of people are invited. This tradition can be sampled in city restaurants, manor house restaurants, on luxurious ferry cruisers, and at inns.

— herring salad; tomato and onion salad; Italian salad; cucumber salad; pickles; chicken salad; beets; white or red cabbage; potato salad; mushroom salad; fish salad; radishes.

There's also usually a cheese tray on the smörgåsbord table with:

— at least three different kinds of cheese, for example, emmenthal; camembert; roquefort; Finnish country cheese (for instance, egg cheese); tilsit; crackers and crispbread of various types; pears; apples; and grapes.

The smörgåsbord is truly economical — if you're hungry. Because after you've finished with the buffet, there's the main course, sometimes big, sometimes small:

— Karelian stew; chicken; roast veal; reindeer stew; breaded veal cutlet; omelet.

If the restaurant has a real banquet table, there's also a traditional casserole:

— potato; carrot; rutabaga; Baltic herring and potato; salmon; macaroni.

Maksapasteija
Liver pâté

(2 large loaves)

1 kg ground liver (beef or venison)
3—4 onions
3—4 tbsp butter
2 1/2 dl dried breadcrumbs
8 dl milk or milk mixed with cream
5 eggs
6 tsp salt
2 tsp white pepper
1—2 tbsp brandy
1—2 cloves garlic
(1—2 tbsp crushed dried mushrooms — chantarelle, cep, or morel)
bay leaves

1. Dice the onions and fry gently in butter.
2. Soak the dried breadcrumbs in the milk.
3. Stir the eggs only long enough to blend yolk and white.
4. Mix all the ingredients and season as you like.
5. Grease two large loaf pans or several small baking dishes. Pour in the mixture and decorate with a few bay leaves.
6. Put the dishes onto a roasting pan and cover the bottom with water. Bake for c. 1 1/2 hours at 175°C.

Lindströmin pihvi
Hamburger à la Lindström

300 g ground beef
300 g boiled potatoes
300 g boiled beets
2 eggs
salt, white pepper

Accompaniment:
onion rings

1. Put the potatoes and beets through a meat grinder or food processor.
2. Mix all the ingredients in a bowl. Add salt and pepper to taste.
3. Form the mixture into flat burgers and fry them in butter until golden brown on both sides. The mixture sticks easily, so make sure the pan isn't too hot!
4. Fry the onion rings on another pan: brown first and then cover and simmer gently. If you like sweet things, add some syrup and a bit of water.
5. Heap the onions on top of the burgers and serve. And remember: there is no such thing as too much onion!

Lihapullat
Meatballs

500 g ground meat (2/3 beef, 1/3 pork)
1 dl dried breadcrumbs
2 — 2 1/2 dl water or water and cream
1 small onion, grated
1 1/2 tsp salt
white pepper
(thyme, garlic)
1 egg

To fry:
butter, margarine, or oil

1. Soak the breadcrumbs in the liquid to swell.
2. Add the other ingredients and beat well.
3. Season with salt and pepper, and add other seasonings if you like.
4. Mould the meat into meatballs with wet hands.
5. Fry in fat until golden brown and done all the way through.
6. Serve hot or cold.

Uunikermasilakat
Creamed Baltic herring casserole

(serves 6)

1 kg Baltic herring fillets
2 dl sour cream
3 dl thick cream
1 can anchovy fillets
a bunch of dill
1 onion
2 tbsp butter
salt, white pepper
dried bread crumbs

1. Dice the onion and simmer in butter. Spread over the bottom of an oven-proof baking dish. Lay the Baltic herring fillets out on a board; season lightly. Place half an anchovy fillet on each herring fillet. Roll the herrings and arrange them in the baking dish.
2. Mix the two creams. Pour half of the liquid onto the fish rolls. Bake at 175°C for c. 40 minutes.
3. When the herrings are tender, pour the accumulated broth into a pot. Add the rest of the cream and a bit of flour to thicken it. Check the flavor and add finely chopped dill.
4. Pour the mixture back onto the herring rolls. Sprinkle with dried bread crumbs and let the casserole brown quickly at 225°C.
5. Serve with mashed potatoes topped with a pat of butter or with boiled potatoes.

Kalahyytelö
Fish in aspic

1—1/2 kg bream, pike perch, or rainbow trout
(a bit of smoked fish)
water, salt (1 tbsp/liter water)
1/4 tsp whole allspice
large onion, quartered
2 bay leaves
1 tbsp white vinegar or white wine vinegar

Aspic:
6 dl fish broth
5 gelatin leaves (or 1 envelope unflavored gelatin powder)

1. If you use bream or pike perch, scale and clean the fish. Rainbow trout is usually already cleaned and needs nothing more than a wipe with a paper towel.
2. Cut the fish into large pieces and place them, the spices, and the onion in a large pot. Add enough water to cover the fish well.
3. Simmer the fish gently for half an hour, checking the broth after a few minutes and adding extra spices if necessary. Let the fish cool in the broth.
4. Remove the flesh from the bones and be sure to do a good job! Arrange the flesh in a suitable dish. You can add boned smoked fish if you like, to give it more taste.
5. Soak the gelatin leaves for a few minutes in cold water to soften them, then press out excess water. If you are using gelatin powder, follow the directions on the envelope. Set aside 6 dl of fish broth. Take 1 dl of this broth, bring it to a boil and melt the gelatin leaves in it. Add the remaining 5 dl. Pour this aspic over the fish.
6. Jell in a cool place.
7. Serve with freshly boiled potatoes, lettuce, and mayonnaise seasoned with herbs.

Sinappisilakat
Herrings with mustard dressing

1 kg Baltic herrings or 600 g Baltic herring fillets

Marinade:
5 dl water
1 dl white vinegar
2 tsp salt
Mustard dressing:
3 tbsp mustard, 1/3 of it French mustard
3 tbsp sugar
2 tsp salt
2 tsp white vinegar
3/4 dl water
1 dl cooking oil
plenty of chopped dill

1. Fillet the herrings, skinning or not. Cut them lengthwise in half.
2. Mix the marinade and pour it over the fish. Let the fillets marinate for 3—4 hours.
3. To make the mustard dressing, mix together the mustard, sugar, salt, vinegar, and water. Add the oil gradually, beating well.
4. Drain the herring fillets thoroughly.
5. Place alternate layers of herring fillets, chopped dill, and mustard dressing in a jug or jar.
6. Cover and refrigerate at least one day before serving.
7. Serve with boiled or baked potatoes, or with rye bread.

Kurkkusalaatti
Cucumber salad

1 large cucumber
1/2 tsp salt
1—2 tbsp sugar

Marinade:
1/2 tbsp white vinegar
1 dl water
chopped dill

1. Rinse the cucumber and slice it finely.
2. Put into a deep dish and sprinkle with salt and sugar. Cover with another dish and shake the slices between the two until the slices are almost transparent.
3. Mix the water and vinegar. Pour over the cucumber slices. Sprinkle with chopped dill.
4. Keep in a cool place if not to be served immediately.

Local Delicacies

One should always take advantage of local specialties. In Northern Karelia, for instance, there are Karelian pasties and "egg butter." In Savo, it's vendace, either plain, baked in a rye bread shell, or in a stew. The buffet specialists on ships are especially proud of their range of shrimp.

The best cooks know how to adapt international ideas to Finnish foods. You'll notice this in the various smörgåsbords. They have international features, typically Finnish foods (herring salads, salt fish, meat jellies), and local dishes.

If you go through Finland with your eyes open and without reserve, you won't have to be satisfied with the ordinary. And you certainly won't go hungry, either.

Kotijuusto
Home-made cheese

3 l milk
1 l buttermilk
3 eggs
salt

1. Whip the buttermilk and eggs.
2. Heat the milk, and when it boils, add the buttermilk and egg mixture, beating well.
3. Turn off the heat, but let the pot stay on the burner until the liquid forms at the top and the cheese settles to the bottom.
4. Line a cheese mould or a strainer with gauze and ladle the cheese in with a slatted spoon.
5. Sprinkle salt between the layers.
6. Cover the mould or strainer with a plate or other weight. Store in a cold place and serve the following day.

Local specialties have spread around the country. This homemade cheese is made of milk, buttermilk, and eggs.

56

Patakukko
Fish pie

1 kg small perch or vendace
250 g fatty pork
1 1/2 — 2 tbsp salt
a drop of water

Pie dough:
rye flour
water
salt

1. Clean the fish and sprinkle with salt. Let the fish sit for a couple of hours or overnight to let the salt soak in.
2. Place the fish in a greased baking dish and add a drop of water.
3. Make a compact dough of the rye flour, salt, and water, and cover the dish with it.
4. Bake in a 150—175°C oven for 2—3 hours.

Kalakukko
Fish pasty

1. Use the same ingredients as for **Patakukko — fish pie.**
2. Make double the amount of dough and knead it well on a floured board. Roll the dough into a sheet c. 2 cm thick, preferably right on baking paper, making it easier to transfer the dough to a cookie sheet for baking.
3. Sprinkle the dough with rye flour and then stack with alternate layers of fish and pork, with salt sprinkled in between. The top layer should be pork.
4. Lift the sides of the dough onto the filling and make a "package" making sure that it is smooth and has no holes.
5. Bake the pasty first at 275°C, to brown it, then reduce the temperature to 150°C and bake for 4—5 hours. Baste now and then with melted lard.
6. If the pasty begins to "sing" — if it starts to leak! — plug up the holes with a bit of dough to keep the juices inside.
7. When the pasty is ready, take it out of the oven, wrap it in foil and then in a thick towel. Let it stand for another half an hour.
8. Serve hot or cold with butter and with buttermilk or milk to drink.

The Finns' basic diet includes milk, potatoes, bread, meat, and fish, but this combination varies from one part of the country to the next. We can speak of regional foods, the traditions of different districts. Improved communications and urbanization have, however, made cuisine more homogeneous, resulting in mixtures of types and a loss of some traditions.

Finland's location is also gastronomically interesting: there have been strong influences from both east and west. At one time it was easy to draw a "bread and buttermilk line" through Finalnd, since in the west, people baked rarely, but a lot at a time, and their buttermilk was long and stretchy. In the east, people baked at least once a week and made pasties in addition to bread, and the buttermilk was "short" and more clotted.

Karelia, in eastern Finland, is the home of pasties, filled with rice or potatoes, and of Karelian stew.

Savo, west of Karelia, is best known for its fish pasty, *kalakukko.* This pasty can also be filled with rutabaga and pork instead of fish. The Savo dish *tirripaisti* is fried pork with potatoes, while *kopratalkkuna* is a thick porridge made from various kinds of flour.

An ingenious shell or lunch box of yore. You can eat the shell, or crust, as well as the fish and pork that have been baked inside it.

Ostrobothnia, on the west coast, is famous for its *bread cheese.* In olden days, milk was preserved for the winter in the form of cheese: it was drawn and formed into round, bread-like slabs which were toasted before the fire before serving, until they were speckled brown. In Ostrobothnia, as well as in Lapland, bread cheese is eaten crumbled into coffee. A *real* bread is the Ostrobothnian *rieska,* a flat, unleavened barley loaf.

The people of the province of *Häme* specialize in "buttermilk cheese" and what is called "lump soup," where the lumps — or dumplings — are made of potatoes, flour, eggs, and seasonings and float around decoratively in meat soup. Häme is the

Among everyone's favorite traditional dishes are meatballs, Karelian stew, and fish and meat stew. In the forefront "Lemin särä," lamb baked in a hollowed-out log.

58

Oversize, lace-brimmed pancakes, muurinpohjaletut, are fried in cast-iron pots and frequently sprinkled with sugar. You can also enjoy them with fish and other savory fillings that go well with the barley in the dough.

Karjalanpaisti
Karelian stew

1/2 kg beef
1/4 kg mutton
1/4 kg pork
1 calf kidney
250 g liver
(1 onion)
1/8—1/4 tsp whole allspice
1 tbsp salt
water

1. Trim the meat and cut into pieces.
2. Place the meat and spices in layers in an oven-proof casserole, with the pork topmost.
3. Add enough water to cover.
4. Bake in a hot oven (225°C), first without a lid, to brown the meat. Then cover and reduce the temperature to 175°C. Bake for 2—3 hours.

home of *sahti,* a strong home-brewed beer. For dessert, after all the famous casseroles, there's raisin pudding or soup.

The inhabitants of *Satakunta* nail whitefish to boards and broil them golden, sizzling brown. The same area produces goat cheese, grilled lampreys, and a type of sweet pretzel, the *rinkeli,* from Eura. Barley groat porridge is a festive dish, baked for a long time and turning pink in the process!

In *Finland Proper,* the southwest, various types of sausage are common, and in the province of *Uusimaa,* they make potato porridge. In this part of Finland, vegetables are served more often and with greater imagination than elsewhere in the country.

Lapland is exotic even to the Finns. All of Lapland — and that includes Santa Claus — lives on reindeer meat: smoked roast reindeer, reindeer stew, reindeer tongue, reindeer chops, reindeer meat soup,

The new Finnish cuisine serves snow grouse, the game bird of the North, fried until rosy. Traditionally it is well done, served with cream sauce, berries, and pickled mushrooms.

Ahvenanmaan pannukakku
Åland oven pancake

1 l milk
1 dl rice (not the long-grained variety) or semolina (not quick-cooking)
1 dl flour
2 eggs
1 dl sugar
1/2 tsp salt
a bit of cardamom

1. Bring the milk to a boil and whisk in the rice or semolina. Cook for 20 minutes to make a porridge. Cool.
2. Whisk the eggs and sugar and add them to the porridge. Stir in the flour, salt, and a bit of cardamom.
3. Grease a frying or baking pan. Pour in the batter and bake the pancake in a hot oven, 225—250°C, until golden brown.
4. Serve with jam and whipped cream.

**Riekko kermakastikkeessa
Snow grouse with creamy bird sauce**

2 young snow grouse
2 tsp salt
a dash of white pepper

For frying:
butter
3—4 dl good bouillon or water

Sauce:
2 1/2 dl juice from the birds
2 1/2 tbsp flour
2 dl cream
salt
1—2 tsp blackcurrant jelly
(1—2 tsp blue cheese)

1. Fry the cleaned birds in butter.

Sprinkle with salt and white pepper.
2. Add bouillon and cover with a lid. Let simmer approximately 45 minutes until well done.
3. Keep the birds warm.
4. Pour the frying juice through a sieve into a small pan. Mix the flour with cold water and whip it into the juice. Let boil c. 5 minutes. Add cream and seasonings. Let simmer for a couple of minutes.
5. Debone the birds and arrange the pieces of meat on a serving dish. Pour boiling sauce over the meat. Serve with boiled potatoes, jelly or berries, and vegetables.

reindeer meat sausage... When you add salmon caught in the rivers of Lapland, cloudberries, and ptarmigan, you have it made!

The reindeer is a way of life in *Lapland*. It's both a pack animal and the tourist's darling. Its skins are made into boots and furs. Its horns are made into souvenirs. But above all reindeer are the Lapp's *cattle*. The Lapp lives on and from reindeer meat.

Reindeer meat is wonderful. It has a slightly gamy taste, is rich in nutrients but not too fatty. It's easy to digest and can be served in a variety of ways. The reindeer tastes so good because it eats good food itself: first it's fed on its mother's milk, later it forages for its own moss, in the unpolluted wilds of Lapland.

Reindeer dishes combine old Lapp folk traditions with modern meat technology, quality controls, and inspections.

You can make anything out of reindeer meat, from soup to stews. But Lapland has its own delicious specialties.

The Lapp serves smoked reindeer roast in thin slices as an appetizer and on sandwiches. Reindeer tongue is delicious cooked and also makes an excellent pâté.

One of the simplest, tastiest, and perhaps most famous reinder dishes is *reindeer stew*. The meat is cut into slivers while still frozen, put into a pot with a bit of water, and simmered until tender. Experts have different views of what "real" reindeer stew should be. Some say that fatty pork should be added to the pot. It's a matter of taste. The stew is served with mashed potatoes, seasoned with butter and onions, and lingonberry purée. (Some purists leave that out, too.)

Reindeer meat has its own special taste and doesn't need any "fancy" spices. The most common seasonings are green and black pepper, allspice, bay leaves, and salt. Suitable accompaniments are onions, carrots, celery, parsnips, and pickled cucumbers. Reindeer meat doesn't suffer if you cook it with cream or sour cream, either. It also gets along well with mushrooms and berries: lingonberries, cranberries, rowanberries.

There are reindeer cutlets, steaks, meatballs, liver (which makes an excellent casserole together with rice and raisins). Reindeer saddle looks festive on any dinner table. And reindeer tartare? Of course. Those who love raw meat should try marinating reindeer instead of beef! There's nothing better.

Poronkäristys
Reindeer stew

1 kg boneless, frozen reindeer
— roast or shoulder
100—200 g lard or butter
water
salt
(white pepper, onions)

1. Cut the lard or butter into very small cubes or slivers.
2. Heat the fat well in an iron pot or Dutch oven.
3. Cut the meat into slivers while still frozen. Add the frozen meat to the pot. Cover and simmer.
4. When all the water from the frozen meat has evaporated, the liquid is clear. This is the fat that browns the meat. Add a bit of water to the pot and continue simmering for half an hour or longer, until the meat is tender. You can add onions and white pepper at this stage, if you like.
5. Add salt to taste.
6. Serve the stew with mashed potatoes seasoned with onions simmered in butter.

Puréed lingonberries are a traditional side dish, while jams made from other berries and raw vegetable salads are newer accompaniments.

Perunasose
Mashed potatoes

1 kg potatoes
water, salt
2 tbsp butter
2 dl milk (or 2 dl cooking broth
and milk powder)
(1 tsp sugar)
2 tsp salt

1. Peel the potatoes and boil until tender in a small amount of salted water.
2. Pour off the water. (Reserve it if you use milk powder instead of milk.)
3. Mash the potatoes, add butter, salt (sugar), and scalded milk. Whip until fluffy.
4. Serve immediately.

The reindeer is the cow of Lapland. Everyone in Finland appreciates reindeer stew: thin strips of meat are carved from a chunk of frozen reindeer beef and then simmered in melted snow to make a stew.

Some Specialties

It's common knowledge that a gifted person is also a gifted eater. In other words, great men and women, famous personalities, are often gourmets, lovers of good food. This is true in Finland, where many dishes have been named after the people who ate them. A Finn is an individualist who wants his food made just so, exactly the way he wants it.

Finland's Marshal Mannerheim was a well known gourmet — and very finicky to boot. His glass of schnapps could not be filled any which-way. It had to be filled to the brim, and woe be to the officer at his table whose hand was not as steady as the Marshal's. The Marshal introduced several dishes into the Finnish menu. The most famous is a special delicacy just right as an appetizer or evening snack, *vorschmack,* originally imported from Poland.

Marshal Mannerheim's favorite drink is also famous, under the name *Marskin ryyppy.* This is how to mix it:

> 50 cl Extra Aquavit
> 50 cl *Pöytäviina* or vodka
> 2 cl Noilly Prat vermouth
> 1 cl gin

Put the ingredients into a cocktail shaker and shake! Fill the glasses to the brim.

Vorschmack

1 kg roast lamb
1 salt herring, soaked, or 2 matjes herring fillets
2 onions
butter
roasting
juices from the roast or bouillon
1/2—1 tbsp tomato purée
1—2 tbsp mustard
white pepper
c. 1 dl cream
(a small can of anchovies)

Condiments:
sour cream
diced pickled cucumbers
diced pickled beets

1. Clean and fillet the herrings.
2. Put the roast lamb, herring fillets, and onions through a meat grinder.
3. Melt the butter in a thick-bottomed pot or dutch oven. Add the ground meat mixture and bring it to a boil.
4. Add just enough juice or bouillon to give a porridge-like consistency.
5. Season and add cream. Simmer for 1/2 to 1 hour, or even longer, but be careful not to let it stick!
6. Serve in the pot, with the condiments set out separately.

You can also use vorschmack as a filling for crêpes or an omelet.

A mixture of ground lamb and herring, called vorschmak, is a tasty appetizer or late night snack. It is often served with a glass of ice-cold vodka.

Finland's late President Urho Kekkonen was also a lover of good food. He especially liked the chowder which is a specialty of his native district of Kainuu. To make *Kekkonen's Chowder,* dice some peeled potatoes and put them into hot water. Add quartered onions, a bay leaf, whole allspice, and salt. Cook the potatoes until almost done. Add large pieces of fish: salmon, whitefish, or burbot, and dabs of butter. Simmer until the fish is done. If you like, thicken the soup Kainuu-style with a bit of rye flour, or leave it clear. Sprinkle with plenty of diced dill and chives. Let each person top his or her serving of chowder with finely chopped raw onions and melted butter.

Finland's current President, Mauno Koivisto, now serving his second six-year term, has never revealed his favorite dish, and neither has his wife, Tellervo, who jokes that the President would never be served anything else if she did.

Still, when President Koivisto was head of the Bank of Finland, he told a restaurant publication about his favorite foods. It's not likely that his taste has changed much since. What is surprising is that presidents seem to like the same kinds of things.

"He likes good, well-prepared dishes. He especially likes home-made food, but also likes to eat good food elsewhere. Since a public figure has to do a lot of representation and eat different kinds of meals, home-made, everyday food is quite a delicacy. These include such fish dishes as burbot soup and stew, grilled Baltic herring, baked bream, and stuffed pike. The Koivistos are not especially fond of salmon or sweet desserts. Mauno Koivisto is a devotee of the healthy life..."

At family lunches the president drinks "the President's mixture," buttermilk thinned with homogenized milk.

The Koivistos have a farm in Inkoo called Tähtelä. This is where Tellervo Koivisto makes her own food, her husband's favorites. She says that she especially likes Inkoo's famous potato porridge.

Local specialties aside, Finnish menus are international, especially when it comes to meat. Finland's best known composer, Jean Sibelius, left to posterity not only his music, but also the special ritual which accompanies "his" steak tartare. To get *Sibelius' Steak,* order steak tartare with the usual accompaniments: pickles, beets, diced onions, capers, and a raw egg yolk. Divide the meat into two. Eat one half raw and send the other half back to the kitchen to be broiled. You get a hot dish as well as a cold one!

Inkoon puuro eli perunapuuro
Inkoo porridge or potato porridge

4—5 potatoes
1 l water
1 1/2 dl barley flour
2 tsp salt
1 tbsp butter

1. Peel and slice the potatoes, and put in a pot with water.
2. Cook until done. Sieve off the water but save it.
3. Mash the potatoes, and return the water to the pot.
4. Bring to a boil and whisk in the flour and salt.
5. Simmer for about 20 minutes, then add the butter.
6. Serve with cold milk and a dab of butter.

5

The Eating Day

Breakfast is a full and varied meal. Porridge is popular, and so are cheese rolls. A glass of milk, fruit, or vegetables complete the meal.

Uunipuuro (ohra tai riisi)
Oven porridge from barley groats or rice

5 dl water
5 dl milk
1 1/2 dl barley groats or raw rice
1 tsp salt

1. Put all ingredients in a greased oven-proof dish or ceramic pot.
2. Place in a 180°C oven and bake until done, about 2 hours.

Viili
Clabbered milk

(for 4)

*2 tbsp **viili** culture or ready-made viili*
8 dl lukewarm whole milk, preferably straight from the cow

1. Beat the *viili* culture or ready-made *viili*. If you use the store-bought variety, take some from just below the *viili*'s skinlike surface.
2. Divide the *viili* among four small bowls. Fill up with warm milk.
3. Cover the bowls and keep in a warm place until the next day.
4. If you use whole milk, there will be a layer of cream on the top. When the *viili* has soured and set, put the bowls in a cool place.
5. Serve cold with berries, sugar, *talkkuna* (a mixture of powdered oats, barley, and peas used in Finland especially with *viili*), müsli, dry breakfast cereal, etc.

Morning

"Eat your oatmeal, and you'll grow up big and strong." This is the kind of advice that's drummed into the heads of all Finns at school and on popular children's programs. And people still eat a lot of porridge; oatmeal, cream of wheat, rye flakes, barley, and rice porridge. Of course there is the cold variation: dry cereals of various types.

Many homes regularly deliver the old porridge sermons — as well as good porridge — to emphasize the importance of eating a good breakfast. And plenty of public "propaganda" is produced, too. The Finn gulps down too little in the morning. The most important thing, he says, is to get a cup of coffee. Otherwise he can't get his eyes open and won't dare to go out into the dark. (Remember that the sun still hasn't risen when it's time to go to work or school from November to February.)

Naturally people are aware of the importance of a good breakfast. Some construct their meat and cheese sandwiches in the evening in readiness for the morning. And many do take pains with the breakfast table: there's coffee, tea, or hot chocolate; juice (apple, lingonberry, or black currant); porridge; whole-grain bread, rolls, or toast; cheese; boiled or fried eggs; sausages or ham; honey, butter, jam; fruit. A carton of yogurt or *viili* adds a bit of variety.

The background music to this feast is the rustle of newspapers or the morning chatter of birds. The clock ticks by faster than usual. The radio gives the morning news and weather and plays lively wake-up music. On certain days there are hints to listeners in between the pieces — for instance, about the importance of a good breakfast.

Noon

Lunch in Finland is served early, at noon or perhaps even earlier.

There are as many different kinds of lunches as there are people. The office girl goes to the company cafeteria or the café around the corner, or unwraps a cheese and sausage sandwich, gets a cup of coffee from a vending machine, and peels an orange.

The construction worker eats a hearty lunch of meat soup, bread, butter, and milk at the work-site diner.

The civil servant stops in at a café for a meat pasty and bouillon while the ad man reserves a table at a good restaurant for a business lunch.

The teacher eats the same school lunch as the children. We've come far in Finland in the way of school lunches. The guiding principle is that each school child should get a hot, nourishing, varied meal — one which also tastes good and is worth waiting for during the long school day.

As the distances between job and home increase, few people have time to go home for lunch. The people who do, probably eat "brunch," a heartier from of breakfast.

Lunch is not as important a time for the Finns as it is for the French, for example. It's a break from work, a way to divide the day in two. Lunch time is also a chance to rush out and do some shopping.

And speaking of lunch: one doesn't always have to gobble it down. We haven't quite lost the idea in Finland that life is still a leisurely business.

The "long lunch," or business lunch, does not necessarily mean eating and drinking oneself to death. It can be a session of intensive contact with another person, a successful long debate or discussion between people of different opinions who enjoy one another's company.

A meal with others is one of the humane elements in human life, and one shouldn't have to think about time. Thank goodness you'll still notice in Finland that forgetting the time now and then is a rather important thing...

Kaalikääryleet
Cabbage rolls

a large cabbage
water, salt

Filling:
1 dl raw rice
water, salt
300 g ground beef
the core of the cabbage
1 small onion, grated
1/2 dl dried breadcrumbs
1/2 dl water
1/2 dl cream
salt, black pepper
For frying:
butter, margarine, or oil
On top:
2 tbsp syrup
water or bouillon

1. Dig out the core of the cabbage.
2. Cook the cabbage in salted water until done.
3. Remove the leaves and drain. Pare down the thick base of each leaf.
4. Cook the rice in salted water.
5. Let the breadcrumbs swell in the water and cream mixture.
6. Mix the ground beef, breadcrumbs, onion, seasoning, and rice. Dice the core of the cabbage and add to the ground beef mixture. Season.
7. Spread cabbage leaves on a board. Put 1—2 tbsp of filling on each leaf. Wrap into little packages.
8. Place the packages side by side in a greased baking dish. Top with a few dabs of butter and pour on syrup.
9. Bake at 225°C until slightly brown. Turn and bake some more. Add water or bouillon.
10. Lower the temperature to 180°C. Baste and bake for 45—60 minutes.
11. Serve with lingonberry or cranberry jam or fresh puréed berries.

Stroganoff

1/2 kg tender, boneless beef
2—3 tbsp butter, margarine, or oil
1 onion
salt, white pepper
2 tbsp flour
water
a small can of tomato purée
(a bit of mustard)
c. 1 dl cream
2 pickled cucumbers

1. Cut the meat into thin strips or cubes (2 × 2 cm).
2. Brown the meat in fat in a hot frying pan or pot.
3. Add the diced onion and let it brown a bit.
4. Season and sprinkle with flour.
5. When the flour turns light brown, add water, tomato purée (and a bit of mustard).
6. Cover and simmer until tender.
7. Season once more. Just before serving, add cream and bring to a boil.
8. Cube the pickled cucumbers and sprinkle them over the meat.
9. Serve with potatoes or rice.

Läskisoosi
Pork in gravy

100—150 g fresh or smoked pork (side)
c. 2 tbsp flour
1 onion
hot water
salt, white pepper

1. Cut the pork into cubes and brown in a pan in its own grease.
2. Remove the cubes from the pan and add the flour to brown it.
3. Add finely chopped onion and simmer until transparent. Then pour in enough boiling water to make a smooth sauce.
4. Return the meat to the pan. Simmer until the meat is done.
5. Season and, if you like, add a dash of mustard, catsup, or other condiment.

Dinner and Supper

"Dinner" sounds rather elaborate to the Finn. On weekdays he rarely eats "dinner" at home, he just has a simple one-course meal around 5 p.m.

Dinner means dressing up, long tables set elegantly at a restaurant, rows of glasses, and long, formal speeches — a Scandinavian vice. Dinners are held for family reunions, a good business year, an "advanced" age (50, 60, 70, 75, 80, etc.), as part of club acitivities, PR, and politics.

Dinners can also be held at home. People rarely speak of "dinners" then. They just say, "Come on over" or "Come have something to eat with us tomorrow" or "Come have some crayfish." Friends arrive and know that they'll get food made with care by the lady of the house. They come in, hand her a bunch of flowers or a bottle of wine, and sit down to enjoy the evening.

The evening progresses in different ways, depending on the situation and the host. Some start off with an aperitif. Others try to get the party going right away by mixing strong cocktails, while others ration the alcohol throughout the evening. In any case, the volume gets louder as the night wears on and the Finn isn't really as shy and as much of an introvert as the guide books say he is.

On weekday evenings, the guests ask to have a taxi called (drunken driving is illegal, of course, and one stiff drink is too much) at about midnight or one o'clock at the latest. On a night before a day off, the party can go on till morning.

In this case, the lady of the house decides that it's been quite a while since dinner, and a midnight snack might be a good idea. It's often anchovies or Baltic herring casserole, herring, sausage, cheese, onion soup, or borsch. Drinks are shot-glasses of vodka and tall glasses of beer — a combination which can prove distressing since wine was served earlier in the evening.

Tea and sandwiches

On weekday evenings, many families serve tea. Every member of the family knows that tea time is eight thirty, for example, time for a pleasant evening gathering. Maybe not everyone has time, so a tea cozy is put on the pot to keep it warm. Tea is accompanied by sandwiches, cookies, rusks and jam, rolls, pasties, pizza. Warm cheese sandwiches are also good with tea.

Finnish sandwiches at their best are open-faced, fairly simple affairs made with dark bread.

At some cafés in the countryside, or at service station cafeterias, you might get sandwiches which might not be very elegant, but at least are big. And most important of all, they're made with whole-wheat bread and sure to be fresh.

In the mornings, the best cafés have soft rolls of different sorts, for instance whole-wheat rolls with cheese, a good energy snack. Any restaurant will make sandwiches to order, on dark bread or light.

At some stage of his visit, the tourist is always served *patakukko* or *kalakukko,* fish pasty. It isn't a sandwich, though it was originally used in packed lunches. It's a hearty, delicious food which keeps well.

The *kalakukko* is in fact an excellent creation of a vivid imagination: someone had to think up a good covering for an easily spoiled food. The result is a treat which looks like a loaf of bread and has a comic name. *Kala* means fish, and *kukko* means cock. No one knows where the name came from or who invented this masterpiece.

The casing of the *kalakukko* is made of rye flour dough. The filling is alternate layers of vendace or small perch and fatty pork. The filling is sealed in the dough and this "cock" is baked in the oven. Inside the casing, the fish and fatty meat melt into a delicious blend and the fish bones just seem to evaporate. The *kalakukko* is sliced, its shell spread with butter, and the fish filling stacked on top. It's a great portable snack, evening treat, or even main dish, filling and warming. The *kalakukko* can be heated up later on and tastes just as good or better.

Kaalipiirakka
Cabbage pasty

Crust:
8 dl flour
400 g butter or margarine
10 tbsp cold water
1 tsp vinegar
Filling:
1 1/2 — 2 kg white cabbage
a bit of butter or margarine
water
salt, white pepper
syrup

1. Measure the flour onto a baking board, and cut in the butter or margarine with a pastry blender, two knives, or your fingertips until granular.
2. Put the mixture into a bowl, add the water and vinegar, and mix quickly into a dough. Don't knead too much or the dough will get tough.
3. Let the dough stand in the refrigerator while the filling is being prepared.
4. Slice the cabbage with a sharp knife.
5. Brown the slices lightly in a heavy pot, add spices, and simmer the cabbage to soften. Add syrup to taste. Let the mixture cool.
6. Roll out the dough, fold over a couple of times and roll out again, as you would puff pastry. Divide the dough into two parts.
7. Roll out one part into a thin sheet on a baking pan.
8. Spread the cooled filling onto the crust.
9. Roll out the rest of the dough and place it over the filling and bottom crust as a cover.
10. Pinch the edges closed with a fork or the fingers.
11. Brush with beaten egg, prick with a fork, and bake in a 200°C oven until the bottom is done and the top golden brown.
12. Serve warm.

Karpalojäädyke
Cranberry parfait

2 egg yolks
c. 1 1/2 dl confectioner's sugar
c. 1 1/2 dl cranberry purée
4 dl thick cream

1. Whisk the egg yolks and sugar into a foam.
2. Add cranberry purée.
3. Whip the cream and fold into the cranberry mixture.
4. Taste, and add more sugar if needed.
5. Turn the mixture into a parfait mold or bowl rinsed with cold water and freeze.

You can make a parfait from any kind of Finnish berry. The amount of berry purée used should be increased or decreased, depending on the tartness of the berry.

Dessert

As far as desserts go, the Finns are quite lucky: they're still close to nature. The summer guest might just be told that dessert is "a walk into the forest, to our strawberry fields."

You can enjoy these gems of gastronomy straight from the shrub or bush: strawberries, blueberries, raspberries, and maybe even such rarities as arctic bramble and cloudberry.

The same berries are found in preserved form on restaurant menus. You can get crêpes with cloudberry jam or something a bit less extravagant, like whipped lingonberry pudding or what the Finns call "poor knights" — berry preserve on French toast. If you want to make the knights "rich," top them off with whipped cream.

71

Today's Finn might remember his childhood and whipped lingonberry pudding, *vatkattu marjapuuro,* as he bites into an imported orange, banana, or grape. This whipped pudding — the Finns call it a porridge — is a dream: soft as a cloud, sweetly pink, light, but with a full-bodied flavor. The dish is made of cream of wheat and lingonberry juice, chilled and whipped. It can also be bought ready-made from grocery stores. And clear berry fool, *kiisseli,* can also be bought in instant form. If you want to make berry fool from scratch, you'll need berries and potato starch. Berry fool is either refreshingly tart, if you use cranberries or rhubarb, or very sweet, if the ingredients are strawberries, raspberries, or rose hips. People with stomach troubles put their faith in "blueberry soup." It's thinner than a fool and does the trick for any tummy.

When dried fruit first began to arrive in northern harbors from the south, people dreamed up a couple of desserts which thereafter became "musts" to end festive everyday meals: raisin and mixed fruit puddings. It might sound strange, but these swollen fruits in the middle of a thick sweet liquid taste pretty good even in the middle of summer.

A refined and always successful dessert is the *parfait.* You can make it from any kind of berry, but probably only in Finland will you get these special parfaits: cloudberry, rowanberry, and sea buckthorn.

The rowanberry has a special flavor. The fox didn't covet grapes in Finnish fables. He complained about "sour rowanberries." The flavor in this type of dessert is actually delightfully tart and unique. Rowanberry parfait has won at least one prize in international dessert competitions.

Marjapuuro
Whipped berry porridge

1 l water
2—3 dl lingonberry purée or
1 l diluted, strong cowberry or
cranberry juice
1 1/2 dl farina
1 1/2 dl sugar
1/4 tsp salt

1. Cook the berries and water to make a juice and strain.
2. Sweeten with sugar, add salt, and heat to the boiling point.
3. Whip the farina into the boiling juice and cook c. 20 minutes.
4. Let the porridge cool for a while in a cold water bath, then whip to make a light, pink dessert.
5. Serve cold with milk.

Mehukiisseli
Juice fool

1 l strong, diluted berry or fruit juice
4 tbsp potato flour
sugar to taste

1. Add sugar to the juice and mix in the potato flour.
2. Bring to a boil, stirring all the time, and then take the pot off the burner immediately.
3. Pour into a serving dish and sprinkle with sugar.
4. Serve with milk, cream, or whipped cream.

Luumukiisseli
Prune fool

250 g prunes
1 1/2 l water
1 cinnamon stick
2 dl sugar
1 dl berry syrup
5 tbsp potato flour

To decorate:
whipped cream

1. Rinse the prunes and soak them overnight in the water.
2. Add the cinnamon stick and sugar. Simmer gently for half an hour.
3. Add the berry syrup.
4. Dissolve the potato flour in a bit of water. Take the saucepan off the burner and add the thickening in a steady stream, mixing well the whole time.
5. Bring to a boil once more.
6. Pour into a pretty bowl. Cool.
7. Serve with whipped cream.

Luumukermahyytelö
Prune cream

1 egg
3/4 dl sugar
2 1/2 dl chopped, cooked prunes
2 dl thick cream
2 tsp lemon juice
1 tsp vanillin
5 gelatin leaves (or 1 envelope
unflavored gelatin powder)

Topping:
whipped cream, whole or puréed
prunes

1. Put the gelatin leaves to soak in cold water. Press out excess water and melt the leaves in 1 dl boiling-hot water. If you are using gelatin powder, follow the directions on the envelope.
2. Whisk the egg and sugar into a foam. Add the prunes and gelatin mixture, then the lemon juice and vanillin.
3. Whip the cream and fold it into the other ingredients.
4. Jell in a cake pan or glass bowl.
5. Decorate with whipped cream and whole prunes or dabs of puréed prunes.

Ohukaiset
Pancakes

1/2 l milk or
2 1/2 dl cream and 2 1/2 dl water
or mineral water
1 1/2 dl flour
c. 1 tsp salt
2 eggs

1. Mix the flour and the milk. Add the salt and beat in the eggs. Let the batter stand for a minute before frying.
2. Fry pancakes on a hot pan, greased with butter or margarine.
3. Serve with sweet jam.

To make a sheet pancake from the same batter, pour into a greased baking pan or frying pan and bake at 225°C until golden brown.

Marjasalaatti
Berry salad

1. Mix together various kinds of berries, preferably wild ones, or group them elegantly in a serving dish.
2. Splash with a bit of berry liqueur, for example Arctic bramble or cranberry.
3. Serve with whipped cream or ice cream.

Vadelmacharlotta
Raspberry charlotte

jelly roll cake
raspberry jam

Filling:
2 dl milk
1 1/2 dl sugar
4 egg yolks
1/2 vanilla pod
100 g raspberry purée
5 gelatin leaves (or 1 envelope
unflavored gelatin powder)
1/2 dl raspberry liqueur
2 dl thick cream

1. Spread the jelly roll cake with raspberry jam and roll in the normal way. Wrap in waxed paper and refrigerate until just before needed.
2. Line a mold (flat or curved) with waxed paper or plastic wrap. Slice the jelly roll and cover the sides and bottom of the mold, packing the slices close together.
3. To make the filling, bring the milk, half of the sugar, and the vanilla pod to a boil in a saucepan. Whisk the egg yolks and the rest of the sugar in a bowl. Add the hot milk mixture to the yolks and sugar. Pour this liquid back into the saucepan. Heat, stirring constantly until the mixture thickens, but do not boil. Take off the stove and cool, stirring occasionally.
4. Soak the gelatin leaves in cold water until soft. Press out excess water. Heat a little less than 1 dl water and melt the gelatin in it. If you are using gelatin powder, follow the directions on the envelope.
5. Discard the vanilla pod. Stir together the gelatin, raspberry purée, liqueur, and vanilla mixture.
6. Fold in the whipped cream and pour onto the jelly roll slices.
7. Refrigerate.
8. Turn onto a serving platter, remove the waxed paper, and decorate with whipped cream and raspberries.

Kaura-omenajälkiruoka
Apple and oat dessert

4—5 apples
cinnamon

Topping:
4 dl rolled oats (quick-cooking
variety)
1 dl sugar

75 g butter or margarine

1. Peel, core, and slice the apples.
2. Grease an oven-proof dish and cover the bottom with apple slices.
3. Sprinkle with a bit of cinnamon.
4. Combine the oats and sugar. Melt the fat and add it to the mixture. Spread over the apples.
5. Bake at 200° for c. 25 minutes.
6. Serve with ice cream.

Uunissa paistetut omenat
Baked apples

2—3 medium-sized apples per person
brown sugar or syrup
cinnamon
water

1. Wash the apples well and core them, but do not bore all the way through.
2. Grease an oven-proof dish and place the apples hole side up.
3. Mix the sugar and cinnamon and fill the apples. If you use syrup, pour it into the holes and sprinkle with cinnamon.
4. Pour just enough water into the baking dish to cover the bottom.
5. Bake at 225°C for 20—30 minutes. Tart apples bake more quickly than sweet ones and burst easily.
6. Serve warm with vanilla ice cream or vanilla sauce.

Köyhät ritarit
Poor knights

a slice of French bread or coffee
bread per person
1 egg
3 dl milk
pinch of salt

For frying:
butter or margarine
On top:
lingonberry jam (and whipped
cream)

1. Cut a thick slice of bread for each person.
2. Whip the egg and mix in milk and a pinch of salt.
3. Dip the slices in the milk and egg mixture.
4. Fry until golden brown on boths sides.
5. Serve hot topped with a bit of lingonberry jam. If you top it all off with whipped cream, your "poor knights" become "rich knights."

Excellent cheese

Naturally dessert can be replaced by cheese. Finnish cheese is high quality and famous, suitable for export.

The first cheeses were made at home, since making cheese was actually a tasty way to store milk. When Swiss cheese masters came in a century ago and improved on local specialties, the cheese industry began to grow.

Today Finns regard the emmenthal as their very own cheese. Renowed for its high quality, Finnish emmental has found a good export market, notably in the United States, where it is sold under the brand name of Finlandia Swiss!

Finland doesn't surpass such "old" cheese countries as France in the number of types it produces. Only a score or so of different cheeses are made industrially. But home-made cheeses have remained: soft buttermilk cheese (also called Easter or egg cheese) is found nowhere else. Goat cheese (these wise animals are raised in only a few districts), baked cheese, and crunchy cheese from Ostrobothnia are other specialties.

Larger towns have special cheese stores. Country cheese can best be found in shops and market halls. The respected Cheese Society and the ladies' cheese association, called the Cheese Table, work to improve the Finns' knowledge of cheeses.

Cheese and bread is by far the most popular way to eat cheese. Finns like emmenthal, edam or cream cheese on their open-face sandwich. But habits are changing: a growing interest in dessert cheeses like brie, blue-mold, or fresh cheese spiced with herbs, all made in Finland, shows that the Finn is joining the big cheese eaters with close to 11 kilos per person annually.

The best known Finnish quality cheese are emmenthal and Turunmaa cheese. They are usually made of cow's milk, and so is Finnish brie. Finns often serve their guests a selection of cheeses, accompanied by raw vegetables, fruit, crackers and even gingerbread cookies.

Ostrobothnian bread cheese is matured by an open fire. It is simmered in cream, then served with jam or berries. It is a delicious dessert.

Invitation to a Sauna

"Come on over and have a sauna!"

This most often also means: come over and have something to eat at the same time. Because the sauna makes you hungry and thirsty. In the summertime, you don't even need an invitation, since the sauna is warmed up almost every night and always when there are guests.

The body shouldn't be overtaxed with food before a sauna and a swim. Food after the sauna is set out either in the dressing room or in the room adjoining it, which often has a fireplace. Or actually, "set out" is too elaborate a term for it, since usually one puts out what there is, something simple.

Some sausage-loving Finns cook and eat their sausage in the sauna. This makes sauna-ritual purists furious. They believe that the dimly-lit sauna and its sizzling stones are holy and that there shouldn't be any background noise of steaming, often splitting sausage to disturb it.

Others put their link of sausage into an aluminum foil bag which is then placed on top of the sauna stove rocks. When this sausage is hot and juicy, they eat it with their fingers in the dressing room, washed down with store-bought beer or home-made *kalja* or *sahti*, its close relatives. (Incidentally, it's quite all right to drink it right out of the bottle.)

The best sauna beverage is beer, cold, medium-strength beer. Another favorite is home-made juice from the family's own currants, steamed to a syrup, which is then diluted. In the summertime, especially, *sima* (mead) is a good thirst-quencher.

But from thirst to hunger: sausage is simple enough to be just the thing for a stag sauna evening.

Perunasalaatti
Potato salad

c. 1 kg potatoes
water, salt
an apple
pickled cucumber
onion or leek

Dressing:
1 dl mayonnaise
1 dl sour cream
2 dl thick cream
mustard
salt, black pepper
a bit of tarragon and chervil
a dash of white wine vinegar

1. Boil the potatoes in their jackets in salted water until tender. Cool.
2. Peel the potatoes, slice or dice. Peel and dice the apple. Chop the onion and pickled cucumber.
3. Mix the ingredients and add salt if needed.
4. Whip the cream and add it to the other dressing ingredients. Season to taste.
5. Toss the vegetables and dressing, covering evenly. Pour into a serving dish and keep in a cool place.
6. Serve with any kind of sausage or cold meat.

The most typical after-sauna snack: link sausage with beer.

76

Kotikalja
Home-brewed beer

5 l water
1/2 l malt
3 dl sugar
1/2 tsp fresh yeast or a pinch of
dried yeast
1 tbsp hops

1. Put the malt, sugar, and hops in a big jug.
2. Bring the water to a boil and pour it into the jug. Mix well.
3. Cool the mixture to lukewarm. Dissolve the yeast in a bit of the lukewarm liquid and add to the jug.
4. Keep at room temperature until the beer clearly ferments. This takes about a day.
5. Sieve and bottle the beer.
6. Store in a cool place.
7. The beer is ready the next day.

Beer or home-made beer — an everyday beverage at the table — refreshes after a sauna.

When there are more guests, probably not all of whom are crazy about the sausage and inevitable mustard which accompanies it, one might serve bread, butter, herring, cold smoked fish, smoked ham, cheese, cucumber, tomatoes.

In the room adjoining the sauna you can sit around wrapped in a towel and eat with your fingers. Just remember not to wipe greasy fingers on the terrycloth, or linen though!

After you've eaten, you can sit and gaze at the fireplace, go outside and see the mist settle over the lake, listen to the solitary sound of water birds. In a while, you'll get sleepy. It's time to unstick that birch leaf from your knee, put on pyjamas, and fall into bed for the best sleep of your life.

What's this about a birch leaf? That's right. Perhaps not everyone knows that the birch switch is just as important a part of the sauna as the hot stones and becalmed lake nearby. In fact, it might be the fragrance of birch leaves that gives one the best appetite, and later induces that feeling of well-being and relaxation that follows every good sauna bath.

"Finland, with its eternal smoke screen." One visitor made this comment after counting up how many times he had encountered smoke in one form or another. There's the smoke sauna, of course; smoked Baltic herrings from the Market Place; smoked reindeer, that Lapp specialty; smoked ham on open-faced sandwiches; freshly smoked flounder straight from the fisherman in the archipelago; smoked lamb; smoked salmon; smoked whitefish.

Smoke suits the Finn's palate and his nose. Smoking is something more than just a process for preparing food. It's a ritual, an amusing and highly social way of spending time with the family and friends.

Your host proudly displays the smoking oven he built from bricks with his own hands or ingeniously constructed from tin drums. Those who don't go in for do-it-yourself projects buy a simpler smoking box from the hardware store.

Just about anything can be smoked, and the best part of the process, say some, is that mouth-watering, smoky odor that tells you your delicacy will be ready soon.

Originally smoking was used as a method for preserving food. Even the smoke sauna was used not only for bathing (the smoke was let out before the bathers were let in) but also for drying and smoking grain and meat, for example.

Smoked food is simple fare. It doesn't need any exotic seasonings. Usually salt and dill are enough. The main thing to remember is that the ingredients to be smoked — especially fish — must be fresh. And it's a point of honor for the smoker not to make his specialty too smoky. Smoking should only add a little extra nuance to food with a fine taste of its own.

Baltic herring market days in the autumn: fishermen bring their Baltic herring specialties; fresh, salted, smoked, and marinated in jars. They also sell black bread, sea buckthorn juice, berry preserves, mushrooms, and dried herbs.

The silver of Baltic herring turns into gold when smoked.

The Country of Black Bread

Ruisreikäleivät
Rye bread rounds

First day:
1 l water
25 g yeast
3 pieces of rye crisps or dark rye bread
1 l rye flour
Second day:
2 tbsp salt
50 g yeast
c. 1 1/3 dl rye flour

1. On the first day, dissolve the yeast in the lukewarm water. Crumble in the rye crisps or bread and add the rye flour. Let this sour dough stand in a warm place overnight.
2. On the second day, add the salt, more yeast, and the remaining rye flour to the sour dough and knead until smooth.
3. Let the dough rise in a warm place.
4. Make three round, flat loaves, cutting a hole in the center of each with a glass. Let the loaves rise. Put the cut rounds aside.
5. Prick the loaves with a fork and bake at 225°C for c. 25 minutes.
6. Be sure to bake the "holes," too, separately, at the same time!

Piimälimppu
Buttermilk loaves

1 l buttermilk
75 g yeast
2 tsp dried preserved orange peel
2 tsp fennel
2 tsp anise
2 tbsp salt
1 1/2 dl syrup
6 dl rye flour
c. 17 dl flour

1. Dissolve the yeast in luke-warm buttermilk. Add the seasonings, salt, and syrup. Add the rye and wheat flours and knead into a smooth dough.
2. Let the dough rise.
3. Form into loaves and prick them with a fork. Bake at 200°C for about 40 minutes.
4. After 20—30 minutes, brush the loaves with water mixed together with a bit of syrup.

Hard, black bread. That's Finnish gastronomy in a nutshell. Finland is "bread land."

Hunger sure is bad if it doesn't disappear with bread, goes the saying. But bread does more than just take away hunger. Hard, black bread is healthy nourishment and also good for the teeth, since one has to bite and bite hard.

Bread in Finland is always linked with rye, that energy-giving grain. There's a saying that rye puts power in your wrists. A waving field of grain is the symbol of the free man and independent pioneer. This field was cleared long before and with great difficulty, so its produce is naturally valuable.

Traditions have been preserved; so have the taste of rye and ways of eating it. Many forms of rye bread still have a hole in the center, just as they did long ago when the loaves were hung on poles above the oven. This hard bread — it naturally dried out as it hung — is the predecessor of all the crisps and rusks enjoyed by Finns today, and is exported as a Finnish specialty all over the world. (The holes, incidentally, are made into miniature breads these days, under the names *Väinämöisen nappeja* or *Lemminkäisen kuplia.*)

When a child comes home from school, the forester from the forest, the housewife from shopping, they all take a loaf of bread, cut off a slice, spread it with butter — and feel more energetic but also a bit more relaxed. Then maybe they cut another slice and look into the refrigerator to see if there's anything to put on top of it — cheese, sausage, tomato, pickle.

Traditions and the cultural influence from eastern and western neighbors have changed Finnish bread. In the western regions, bread was baked rarely and the stored bread was eaten little by little as the loaves dried out and hardened.

In eastern Finland, on the other hand, people baked more frequently, about once a week. Today, improved communications, increased urbanization, and a more homogeneous society have made bread traditions more uniform. Finns eat bakery-made bread more and more these days. Sometimes a city-dweller is lucky enough to get a chance to taste freshly baked bread when he visits the country on vacation.

The Finn doesn't walk around with a long stick of

bread under his arm as the French do, but his shopping bag regularly includes crisps, heavy French bread, dark sour loaves, tasty "after-oven bread" — hardened in the oven as it cools down — and perhaps a fresh, soft loaf of whole-wheat bread.

Or various specialties: the traditional round, flat rye bread, crisps of all kinds, buttermilk bread, barley loaf. Rolls are either baked at home or bought for breakfast, and so is ready-sliced bread for toast. Rusks are good with coffee.

Bread is supposed to be a good energy food, and indeed it is. A few years ago, a freshly-baked loaf of whole-wheat bread was flown off to an international bread competition (whole-wheat bread should always be eaten fresh) and it won a gold medal for both its flavor and its nutritional value.

The greatness of bread lies in the fact that it is a natural product. When you hold a loaf, cut it into slices just the right thickness, you're in direct contact with the field of grain, with the miracle of growth and nature.

Ohraleipä
Barley bread
1/2 l milk or water
50 g fresh yeast or 1 package dried yeast
2 tbsp salt
5 1/2 dl barley flour
4 1/2 dl flour

1. Warm the milk or water to room temperature and dissolve the yeast and salt in it.
2. Whip in the barley flour and let it sit in a warm place for about an hour.
3. Add the flour and knead until smooth.
4. Let rise.
5. Form into two round loaves. Use plenty of flour, since the dough will be soft.
6. Let the loaves rise.
7. Prick the loaves with a fork and bake at 250°C for 25 minutes.

Grahamsämpylät
Graham rolls
2 1/2 dl milk
25 g yeast
2 tsp salt
1/2 dl syrup
2 dl flour
3 1/2 dl graham flour
50 g butter

1. Dissolve the yeast in the lukewarm milk and add the salt and syrup. Mix in the flours and finally the softened butter and knead into a smooth dough.
2. Let the dough rise.
3. Form into rolls and let them rise again.
4. Bake at 225°C for 10—12 minutes.

Grahamkorput
Graham rusks
3 dl milk
25 g yeast
1 1/2 tsp salt
1/2 dl syrup
c. 6 dl graham flour
100 g butter

1. Make the dough, following the same procedure as for *Graham rolls*.
2. Bake the rolls for only 8—10 minutes.
3. When the rolls have cooled a bit, split them with a fork.
4. Brown and dry the rolls in the oven, at 50°—70° C° overnight (the oven door should be open).

Kaurasämpylät
Oat rolls
2 1/2 dl milk
1 tsp salt
2 tbsp syrup
30 g yeast
2 tsp ground anise
4 dl quick-cooking rolled oats
c. 4 1/2 dl flour
50 g butter

1. Dissolve the yeast in warm milk and add the salt, sugar, and anise. Mix in the oats, flour, and finally the butter.
2. Let the dough rise until double in bulk.
3. Form into rolls. Let them rise again and bake at 225° for 5—8 minutes.
4. Serve immediately while still warm or heat later.

There is an endless variety of breads, prepared with rye, wheat, barley, or oats. Hard crust, soft crust, loaves, rolls, dark bread, white bread, pasties. Bread is an honored food.

Pastries, Pasties, and Pies

Pastries, pasties, and pies are baked at the same time as bread. The best are made at home, preferably in a hot wood-fired oven, but you can also buy them at cafés, at market places, and kiosks.

"Bouillon and a pasty" is many people's idea of a good lunch. Here the pasty is either a greasy, meat-filled boiled concoction or a baked puff pastry filled with meat, egg, and rice or mushroom and rice.

A classic food is the Karelian pasty, whose crust is made of water, salt, and rye flour. The dough is rolled thin and filled with rice or barley porridge or mashed potatoes. The skills needed for making these pasties are respected and difficult to acquire. The rolling, especially, is something that not everyone is able to master. The result must be thin and crisp.

The best Karelian pasties are found in market places in eastern Finland, sold from boxes lined with waxed paper. The pasty is best hot from the oven, but is also good warmed up or even cold. The pasty was originally an important and handy portable lunch and excursion food.

The *sultsina* is a variation of the Karelian pasty, filled loosely with rice porridge or cream of wheat.

"Sheet pasties" are baked, as the name indicates, in sheets. There's a puff pastry crust filled with a mixture of rice, onion, and meat or rice, salmon, and hardboiled egg. Some people fill them with steamed cabbage.

Cooked pasties are made with yeast dough and mostly filled with rice and meat. The dough is set to rise, the mixture is wrapped inside, and the pasty is boiled in fat like a doughnut. These are the ones found at hotdog stands.

Colorful summer delicacies are pies made of rhubarb, lingonberry, blueberry, raspberry, and apple which are not round like "traditional pies." Instead, they're baked in sheets or various other shapes. They're mostly coffee bread dough filled with sweet jams. There's also a type of cheesecake with this kind of crust, a specialty of eastern Finland and well worth trying.

Vatruskat
Potato pasties

1 kg potatoes
1 1/2 dl flour
1/2 tbsp salt

Filling:
cooked rice
butter

1. Peel the potatoes and boil them in salted water.
2. Mash the potatoes and add flour and salt.
3. Form the dough into little balls and flatten them with floured hands into round pasties about 10 cm in diameter.
4. Add some melted butter to the rice and put a bit of the filling into the center of each potato pasty. Fold the pasties over into half moons. Press the edges together and put on a cookie sheet.
5. Prick the pasties with a fork. Bake at 300°C for c. 10 minutes until golden brown.
6. Brush with melted butter.

Perunarieskat
Potato bread

1/2 l mashed potatoes
1 tsp salt
1 egg
c. 2 1/2 dl barley flour

1. Add the salt, egg, and barley flour to the mashed potatoes, which should not be too soft.
2. Divide the dough in two. Flour your hands well and pat the dough into two flat loaves on a cookie sheet covered with baking paper. The loaves should be between 1/2—1 cm thick. You can also make several small loaves c. 10 cm in diameter.
3. Bake at 275°C for 15—25 minutes.
4. Serve hot with butter.

The rich Finnish pastry tradition is inherited from the East. Here are potato pasties, blueberry and lingonberry pie in a rye crust, and potato   pasties.

Karjalanpiirakat
Karelian pasties

(12—14 large pasties)

1 dl water
1 tsp salt
c. 2 dl rye flour
1/2 dl flour

Filling:
1 l milk
2 dl uncooked short-grained rice
salt
To moisten:
melted butter or butter and water

1. Add the flour and salt to the water and mix into a solid, compact dough.
2. Heat the milk and sprinkle in the rice. Simmer for at least 20 minutes to make a thick porridge. Season with salt.
3. Form the dough into a bar and divide into 12—14 or more parts.
4. Roll into balls and flatten into cakes.
5. Sprinkle table and hands with rye flour. Roll the cakes into thin sheets with a rolling pin, thin enough, as the saying goes, "to see seven churches through it."
6. Spread some filling on each sheet, turn the edges partly over the filling, and press to close.
7. Put on a baking sheet and bake in the hottest possible oven.
8. When the bottom of the pasties is slightly browned and the rice filling has a few brown spots, the pasties are ready.
9. Brush them well with melted butter or a butter and water mix-

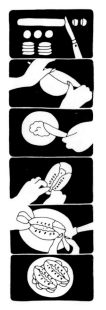

ture.
10. Place the pasties, separated with baking paper, in a bowl and cover with a towel to soften the crusts.
11. Serve warm with "egg butter."

Munavoi
Egg butter

150 g butter
2 hardboiled eggs

1. Soften and cream the butter.
2. Chop the eggs finely and mix with the butter to spreading consistency.

Modern version: Use cottage cheese instead of hardboiled eggs.

Juusto-sienipiirakka
Cheese and mushroom quiche

Crust:
150 g butter
2 dl flour
1 dl grated cheese
2 tbsp cold water
Filling:
3 dl fried mushrooms (horn of plenty, chantarelle, morel, champignon)
1 dl onion, chopped finely and simmered golden in butter
salt, black pepper
1/2 tsp dried or 1 tbsp fresh basil
2 eggs
1 dl cream
1 dl milk
1/2 tbsp flour
2 dl grated cheese

1. To make the crust, combine the flour and grated cheese. Cut the butter into the flour mixture with two knives, a pastry blender, or your fingertips. When the mixture is granular, add the water and toss quickly into a dough. Press the dough onto the bottom and sides of a pie plate.
2. Keep the pie shell in a cold place while you make the filling.
3. Mix together the fried mushrooms and onion, season with salt, black pepper, and basil.
4. Beat the eggs, and add the cream, milk, grated cheese, and flour.
5. Bake the pie shell at 225°C until light brown. Remove from the oven.
6. Pour the filling into the pie shell and bake until the filling is set and golden brown.
7. Serve warm.

Lihapiirakka
Meat pasty

Crust:
3 dl flour
2 dl mashed potatoes
100 g soft butter or margarine
1 tsp baking powder
Filling:
400 g browned ground beef
3 dl cooked rice
1 dl browned diced onion
salt, white pepper
1 dl cream or bouillon
On top:
beaten egg

1. Put the ingredients for the crust in a bowl and mix with the hands, but not too much, or the dough will be tough.
2. Let the dough stand in a cold place for a few minutes.
3. Mix the filling ingredients.
4. Roll the dough into a sheet c. 30 × 54 cm.
5. Spread the filling within 20 cm of one side of the crust.
6. Turn the empty side of the crust onto the filling and press down the edges.
7. Brush with beaten egg and prick with a fork.
8. Bake at 225°C for 25—30 minutes.

Muna-riisi pasteijat
Egg and rice filled pasties

1. Use puff pastry or meat pasty dough. Roll it into a sheet.
2. Cut small round cakes using a glass or cutter.
3. Fill with a mixture of boiled rice, chopped hardboiled eggs, salt, and a sprinkling of cream.
4. Seal the edges together with a fork, forming a pouch. Brush with egg and bake at 225 °C until brown.

Pulla
Coffee bread

1 1/2 dl milk
25 g yeast or 1/2 package dried yeast
1 egg
1 tsp salt
1 dl sugar
1/2 tbsp crushed cardamom
c. 1/2 kg flour
100 g butter or margarine

1. Dissolve the yeast in luke-warm milk.
2. Beat the egg and add to the liquid.
3. Mix in the salt, sugar, cardamom, and flour and beat well.
4. Soften the butter or margarine and add it to the other ingredients. Knead the dough until it separates from the sides of the bowl.
5. Let the dough stand at room temperature for about half an hour. Form into small rolls or long loaves.
6. Let rise. The bread is ready for the oven when you press the surface and the depression bounces back. Brush with beaten egg.
7. Bake loaves at 200°C for 20—25 minutes and rolls at 225°C for 5—10 minutes.

Voisilmäpullat
"Butter eyed" rolls

Form the coffee bread dough into little rolls and let them rise. Brush with beaten egg. Make a hole in each with a finger, pressing all the way down to the bottom of the roll. Put 1/2 tsp butter into each hole. Sprinkle with sugar (and vanillin, if desired).
   Bake at 225°C for 10—23 minutes.

Munkit
Finnish doughnuts

Make the dough for coffee bread, but use slightly less flour. Form into small rolls and let them rise, covered with a cloth or plastic wrap. Cook the doughnuts in hot vegetable oil or coconut oil (180°C) for about 15 minutes, depending on size, or until golden brown. Drain the doughnuts on absorbent paper. Roll in sugar while still warm.

Korvapuustit
Cinnamon buns

1. Use the same recipe as for *Coffee bread.*
2. Roll the dough into a sheet about 1 cm thick.
3. Spread the dough with a thick layer of melted or very soft butter. Sprinkle with sugar and cinnamon. If you like, you can add a layer of chopped or ground almonds or other nuts.
4. Roll and cut into slices c. 3 cm thick.
5. Arrange the slices on a baking sheet covered with baking paper. Let rise.
6. With a finger or the handle of a knife, make a vertical depression down each bun so that the spiral-like filling bulges out on both sides.
7. Let the buns rise. Brush with beaten egg and bake at 225°C for 8—10 minutes.

Rahkapiirakka
Cream cheese pie

Crust:
2 dl milk
75 g butter
1/2 dl sugar
1 tsp salt
1 egg
25 g fresh yeast or 1/2 package dried yeast
6 dl flour
Filling:
2 1/2 dl cream cheese or curd
1 dl sugar
1 dl cream
1 egg
1/2 dl raisins
1/2 tsp vanillin
juice of 1 lemon

1. Cream the butter and sugar. Add the egg and beat well.
2. Dissolve the yeast in lukewarm milk. Add this liquid and salt to the butter mixture.
3. Add the flour gradually. Knead well and let rise.
4. Turn onto baking paper and roll into a sheet about 1 cm thick. Let rise again.
5. Combine all of the ingredients for the filling and stir until smooth.
6. Spread the filling evenly over the crust and bake at 200°C for about 30 minutes.

Lusikkaleivät
Spoon cookies

200 g butter
1 1/2 dl superfine sugar
2 tsp vanillin
250 g flour
1 tsp baking soda

1. Brown the butter in a clean frying pan. Pour it into a bowl and add the sugar. Mix until the butter cools, but do not whisk into a foam.
2. Combine the dry ingredients and add them to the butter mixture.
3. Press bits of dough into the bowl of a teaspoon and turn the spoon-shaped cookies onto a cookie sheet covered with baking paper.
4. Bake at 200°C until light brown. Cool.
5. Put two cookies together with jam. Careful! They break easily!

Kauralastut
Oatmeal cookies

(c. 30)

50 g melted butter or margarine
2 dl rolled oats
1 1/2 dl sugar
1 tbsp flour
1 tsp baking powder
1 egg

1. Melt the butter or margarine and cool slightly.
2. Combine the oats, sugar, flour, and baking powder.
3. Add the melted fat and stir. Beat the egg slightly and add to the batter.
4. Drop the batter by teaspoons onto a cookie sheet covered with baking paper. Leave plenty of space between the cookies, since they spread!
5. Bake for about 6 minutes at 225°C.
6. Let the cookies cool slightly before you remove them from the baking paper and make sure they are completely hard before stacking them in a cookie jar.

Mansikkatäytekakku
Strawberry and cream cake

4 eggs
2 dl sugar
2 dl flour
1 tsp baking powder

Liquid:
c. 1 dl milk or diluted lemon juice
Filling and topping:
1 — 1 1/2 l strawberries
4 dl thick cream
4 tbsp sugar
(1 tsp vanillin)

1. Make a sponge cake, preferably
the day before. Whip the eggs and
sugar into a light foam. Combine
the flour and baking powder and
fold into the egg mixture. Pour into a flat greased and floured cake
pan and bake at 175°C for c. 50
minutes. Let the cake cool slightly
and then turn it out.
2. Split the cake in two or more
layers.
3. Whip the cream until light and
add sugar (and vanillin).
4. Slice about a third of the
strawberries.
5. Moisten the cake with the liquid, using a pastry brush. Spread
with a layer of whipped cream and
strawberry slices. Top with another
layer of cake and repeat the process until all layers are used.
6. Top the cake with whipped
cream and decorate with whole or
sliced strawberries.

Lakkakääretorttu
Cloudberry roll cake

Make a sponge cake dough but
pour it onto a baking sheet
covered with baking paper. Bake
at 225°C for 10—15 minutes until
brown. Turn onto a sheet of paper
sprinkled with sugar. Let cool for
a while. Spread a layer of
cloudberries on the cake and roll it
into a roll cake. Cover with cream
whipped with sugar. Decorate with
cloudberries.

Maustekakku
Soft spice cake

4 dl flour
3 dl sugar
2 tsp ginger
2 tsp cinnamon
2 tsp cloves
2 tsp baking soda
1 1/2 dl lingonberry or apple
purée or jam
1 dl milk powder and 3 dl water
or 3 dl milk
1 1/2 dl melted butter

1. Combine the dry ingredients.
2. Add the purée or jam, water or
milk, and melted butter.
3. Mix quickly into a smooth batter. Pour into a greased and
floured pan and bake at 175°C for
45—60 minutes.

Paraisten piparkakut
Parainen gingerbread cookies

3/4 dl syrup
1 tsp cinnamon
1 tsp ginger
1 tsp cloves
1 tsp dried orange peel
1 tsp salt
150 g butter or margarine
1 dl sugar
1 egg
1 tsp baking soda
c. 6 1/2 dl flour

1. Bring the syrup and spice to a
boil.
2. Whisk the butter and sugar.
Add the warm spice and syrup
mixture and the egg.
3. Add the flour and baking soda,
and mix into a dough.
4. Let the dough stand overnight
in a cold place.
5. Roll out in a sheet 2 mm thick
and cut with a cookie cutter.
6. Bake at 250°C until golden
brown.

Finns frequently serve coffee and
buns. At a more festive coffee
party you can also find snacks.
Small egg and rice-filled pasties
on the left, a cream cheese pie
and cinnamon buns on the plate,
a cloudberry-filled roll cake in the
center. The bowl is filled with
gingerbread cookies. The glasses
have various berry liqueurs in the
glasses.

A Cup of Coffee?

Society in Finland revolves around a cup of coffee. Infants aren't given coffee, and neither are children usually (except sometimes mixed with milk), but at christenings, coffee is a must, just as it is at funerals. In between these two momentous events, many a cup is drunk to celebrate engagements, birthdays, "name days," a new job, retirement.

Finns drink a lot of coffee: about 1300 cups a year per person. No one really asks a guest his preference

in a Finnish home: the coffee pot is put on to boil immediately.

Coffee opens the Finn's eyes in the morning. It's drunk in offices and on construction sites morning and afternoon to keep people going. It's an integral part of meetings and official receptions. Coffee can sometimes even precede a meal, though usually it finishes it.

When does coffee taste best? It's a matter of opinion. Some favor the bed-newspaper-coffee combination, while others think that a fishing or hunting trip is the best setting for a thermos full of coffee.

Coffee is medium-roasted, quite strong, often served with cream or sugar, or both. Coffee helps you keep a clear head through sorrowful times or joyous, when decisions have to be made.

When You're Thirsty

Finns have been brewing beer and distilling liquor for centuries. And there are plenty of sayings about drinking habits. "Have we come here to jabber or to drink?" says one Finn to another, who has dared to propose a toast.

In Finland you don't necessarily have to say *skål* when you raise your glass, or anything else for that matter. Foreigners are, however, for some reason taught that we Finns always say *kippis* or *terve* or *hei* or *hölökyn-kölökyn* — something only a Finn can pronounce.

Since the short experiment with prohibition, alcoholic drinks have been the monopoly of a State company, ALKO.

ALKO tries to instill good drinking habits by launching various campaigns: for moderation, against drunken driving and drinking during pregnancy. It grants funds for research on the effects of alcohol and publishes information on wine and spirits.

ALKO also exports its products. *Finlandia,* the Finnish vodka, is a big success in its famous bottle designed by Tapio Wirkkala. Finlandia is available in the best bars and restaurants throughout the world and also in major tax-free shops at airports and on ships.

Dry Vodka is manufactured from grain. It's colorless and has 38% alcohol by weight (45% by volume). Dry Vodka is most often served with juice, for instance lingonberry, or mixers such as tonic. A

Kahvia suomalaisittain
Finnish coffee

(7 cups)

1 l water
1 1/2 — 2 dl good ground coffee

1. Heat the water and add the coffee.
2. Bring to the boil.
3. Remove from the burner.
4. Let the grounds settle for 3 minutes to let the ground settle.
5. Serve immediately with sugar and cream.

Vodka and vodka-based drinks are served ice-cold. The "icy" bottle was designed by Tapio Wirkkala.

88

mixed drink in Finland is called a *grogi*.

Koskenkorva vodka (also called *Koskis,* or *kossu*) is perhaps the most popular schnapps. This colorless vodka is made from grain, but unlike Dry Vodka, has a bit of sugar and 31.5% alcohol by weight, 38% by volume.

A stiff drink in a small glass is an old Nordic and Slavic tradition. There's the idée fixe that herring, steak tartare, and crayfish simply must be accompanied by schnapps. But of course you can refuse a drink if you're not used to one or if you want to do something *after* lunch, too.

Vodka and Koskis should usually be drunk with something to eat. The wise Russians and Poles emphasize the importance of a snack to accompany the drink: sausage, pickles, mushrooms, small pasties or meatballs.

By the way: if someone wants to make a bet about who knows how to eat a meal backwards, remember to sigh contentedly *before* you down your schnapps!

One common drink with meals is beer. Finland brews good beer, thanks to a long tradition and stiff competition among breweries.

Beer, a popular thirst quencher

There are three types of beer (*olut* in Finnish): *ykkösolut,* or *I olut,* which contains a minimal amount of alcohol and is sold at grocery stores; so is *keskiolut,* also called *III olut,* a medium-strength beer; *A* or *IV olut,* sometimes called export beer, is sold at ALKO only. Medium beer has an alcohol content of 3 – 3.7% by weight (3.9 – 4.7% by volume), while the figures for A beer are 3.7 – 4.5% (4.8 – 5.6%).

Finnish beer is lager beer, with a light color. It's served fairly cold, colder than in British pubs. There's also a Finnish stout, praised by Michael Jackson in his book on beers, and one brand of dark beer.

ALKO has a good selection of wines. In addition to varieties bottled abroad, there are also excellent, moderately priced wines from France, Italy, Spain, Germany, Hungary, Bulgaria, etc. bottled in Finland.

Those who don't drink any alcohol have their reasons. For them there's mineral water, well water, mead, home-brewed non-alcholic beer, etc. Their use has spread considerably, perhaps because drivers in Finland are not supposed to drink anything that contains alcohol before they hit the road. Finnish water is good and the soft drinks made from it are refreshing, especially the range of orange sodas.

At home the Finns steam juices for winter use. Black currant juice is used to combat colds in place of the rum drunk by people in other countries: hot water, sugar, plenty of juice concentrate.

Do the Finns drink a lot? The statistics for annual alcohol consumption changed into liters of pure alcohol are not alarming. We are far from the top of the list.

But, unfortunately, alcohol is a social problem in Finland. Some Finns — heavy drinkers especially — tend to drink too much at one sitting and both sound and look as if they have. The old tradition of buying a bottle of spirits to finish off the work week is still alive. In addition, consumption is growing, as more liquor is served on social occasions.

The finale to a Finnish meal is always coffee. Finland's government trembles before the coffee drinker, wondering when it dares raise the price of coffee again. Coffee is usually drunk with cream and sugar. On a cold day, a Finn might offer his guest a cup of *kahviplörö* (perhaps from the French *café fleur*), coffee with a shot of liquor added. Finnish Coffee is coffee with *Koskenkorva*.

A festive meal is most often topped off with *café avec,* coffee accompanied by a snifter of brandy. Finland is a big importer of French brandies.

Though Finland imports brandies, it exports liqueurs. Instead of grapes, there are Finnish berries, ripened by the short but light summer. The liqueur industry employs both berry pickers and gardeners.

The following liqueurs are definitely worth tasting:
— cloudberry, cranberry, raspberry, arctic bramble, lingonberry, rowanberry, sea buckthorn, strawberry, black currant, apple.

Finland also manufactures sparkling wines made from white currants and gooseberries. Finnish herbs make various types of bitters and aperitifs. You should try the refreshing apple and pear ciders which can be bought at grocery stores. They contain about the same amount of alcohol as medium-strength beer.

Some regions are proud of their *sahti.* This strong, fairly sweet beer is made at home and also sold at ALKO shops in certain traditional *sahti* regions. Especially at hay-making time, housewives in the country brew a milder beer which is a good thirst-quencher.

The traditional May Day drink is *sima,* mead, which can easily be made at home or bought. It's sparkling, sweet, almost honey-like (which in fact is

Washingtonin kotka
Washington Eagle

2 cl vodka
2 cl cloudberry liqueur
2 cl fresh orange juice
1 cl lemon juice
cocktail cherry
blue sugar ring

This cocktail was concocted in honor of President Reagan's visit to Finland in 1988.

The flavour of Finnish berry liqueurs have a lingering flavor.

Aila

2 parts vodka
1 part cranberry liqueur
1 part dry sherry

Stir. Garnish with a
cocktail cherry

Lapin taika
Lapland magic

1 bottle of vodka
10 cl cloudberry liqueur
4 cl lemon juice
5 bottles of soda water
3 dl cloudberries

Stir. Add soda, cloudberries, and
ice just before serving.

what the word *mead* means). *Sima* is also a perfect
after-sauna drink.

What is *spring juice?* That's the sap of the birch.
Traditionally it was a spring delicacy. It was also
used as a health drink, since it contains lots of
minerals, and was a treat for children. There are still
families who tap their birch trees and say spring
juice is good for you. Experts make syrup out of sap
and use it for delicious desserts. The sap is available
in a few health stores.

And how about the best drink of all? Most Finns
would without hesitation answer: *water.* A spring,
well, brook — lovely stops for the thirsty hiker or
back-packer.

Even though the water in some big lakes has been
made unsuitable for drinking by industry, it is still
possible to drink fresh lake water in the wilds, or at
least use it for making coffee and tea. Tap water can
be drunk safely all over Finland, since standards are
very high and controls strict.

Some Habits
of Your Hosts

Leave plenty of time and be prompt. The Finn
usually is. You should make sure you're in no rush,
for instance during an evening out at a restaurant.
Service is never hurried. You will only get a menu by
asking for it politely and when you've read it, it will
be whisked away.

Finns often drink milk with their snacks and
meals. On streets and in parks you can see people
who enthusiastically guzzle down something from
long cartons. This is buttermilk. Very healthy!

If you have a glass of schnapps, the glass is usually filled to the brim. This is not to annoy you.
Remember what we said about Finland's national
hero, Marshal Mannerheim, and his steady hand.

Wines and liquor are not served in restaurants
before the stroke of 11. Only beer is available
before, but only after 9. If you are terribly thristy
for something with a kick, you can buy a bottle
from the nearest liquor store after 10.

If the lady of the house offers you a second help-
ing, have some. She really means it and usually has
plenty in the kitchen. And remember to finish up!
The Finns do.

When Finns go visiting, they take with them either
a plastic bag or a long white paper package. They're

presents for the host and hostess, the former with a bottle of wine, the latter with flowers.

Finnish homes are well heated. But don't take off your suit jacket without asking your hostess' permission.

In winter or the year round during rainy spells, the Finns wear boots or galoshes and so should you! Your hostess will expect you to take them off in the hall and change into shoes or slippers. Bring these along in a handy carrying case or bag.

What to Bring Home

What should I bring home to family and friends when I leave Finland? Hunting knives? Why not.

But you might just think about buying food on your last day here and spend a Finnish evening when you get home. You should finally, if you haven't already done so, go visit the market place or market hall or stop in at a Finnish supermarket. But first a setting for your Finnish evening: The Finns say that a pleasant visual environment is a must. A gastronomic gift can also be something that will last longer than one meal: glassware, a pot, a bowl, a tablecloth.

The Finns make all of these very well. Rural tastes and skills have created a good sense of design and the tradition is continued in glasses, pitchers, bowls, plates, crocks, cutlery, pots and pans. And the materials are all top quality.

The true *pièce de résistance* on a well-set table can be a tablecloth or place mat made of Finnish cotton or linen. Surprising, joyous, subdued, peaceful, colorful — in any shade, but always tasteful. Many international medals and prizes bear witness to the fact that this side of Finnish gastronomy is one of its strongest.

Naturally it's nice if you have time to buy something to fill your table with and the strength to carry your purchases. Fresh food is always difficult to transport unless you're flying. Then you can take anything from freshly picked berries to bread baked that same morning.

If the trip is a long one, better buy jars, bottles, cans. For instance:

— juices, nectars, jams (lingonberry, cloudberry, cranberry, and rowanberry are the most exotic)

— vodka, liqueurs (cranberry, arctic bramble, cloudberry)

Äidin omenakakku
Mother's apple cake

100 g butter or margarine
1 1/2 dl sugar
1 egg
4 dl flour
2 tsp baking powder or 1 level tsp baking soda
1 1/2 dl sour cream
2—3 soft apples

1. Whisk the butter or margarine and sugar into a light foam.
2. Add the egg, beating well, to make a smooth batter.
3. Combine the flour and baking powder/soda. Fold the flour and sour cream alternately into the egg mixture. Don't mix too much or the dough will be tough.
4. Core, peel, and slice the apples.
5. Pour the batter into a tube cake pan and submerge the apple slices.
6. Bake at 175°C for 45—60 minutes.

Kardemummakorput
Little cardamom rusks

200 g butter
1 dl sugar
1 tbsp ground cardamom
5 dl cake flour
3 tsp baking powder
2 dl cream

1. Foam the butter and sugar. Add the ground cardamom.
2. Combine the flour and baking powder. Add them to the mixture alternately with the cream.
3. Let the dough harden for a short time in a cool place.
4. Roll the dough out c. 1 cm thick and cut out small, round cakes.
5. Bake at 225°C for about 10 minutes.
6. Split the warm cakes with a fork.
7. Place, split side up, on a cookie sheet and bake further at 175°C for about 10 minutes. Cool and store in a dry place.

Almost every town has a covered market hall near the market place. These supermarkets of old are sights to see. They offer fresh and tasty things: bread, smoked meat and fish, cheese, and sausages.

— bread, from long-lasting dark bread and crisps to Karelian pasties and loaves

— reindeer meat, ham, various sausages (make sure you follow your country's import regulations and buy canned meats if necessary!)

— herring in various marinades, also vendace, a "Finnish original"

— candies, from chocolate and licorice to pastilles, which the Finns consume by the mountain.

At Easter time you can buy "mignon eggs," real eggshells filled with the finest chocolate nougat, unique to Finland. And if you have the chance, try sugared cranberries.

In the background, play some Finnish music, something truly personal on records or cassettes. Something you won't be able to get at the neighborhood store back home and which your friends will never be able to identify the first time around.

Then top the whole setting off with colorful candles and a good appetite perked up by your pleasant memories.

Index

Ahvenanmaan pannukakku 60
Äidin omenakakku 92
Aila 91
Åland oven pancakes 60
Apple and oat dessert 73
Apples, baked 73

Baked apples 73
Baked bream 15
Baked mutton cabbage 43
Baltic herring fillets 50
Baltic herrings, pickled 20
Barley bread 80
Barley porridge 67
Beer, home-brewed 77
Berry porridge, whipped 72
Berry salad 73
Blinies 37
blinit 37
Blueberry pie 25
Blueberry soup 24
Boiled crayfish 27
Bream, baked 15
Burbot soup 19
"Butter-eyed rolls" 85
Buttermilk loaves 79

Cabbage pasty 70
Cabbage rolls 68
Cardamom rusks 92
Cheese and mushroom quiche 84
Cheese, home-made 56
Christmas ham 40
Christmas tarts 42
Cinnamon buns 85
Clabbered milk 67
Cloudberry roll cake 86
Coffee bread 85
Coffee, Finnish 88
Cranberry parfait 71
Crayfish, boiled 27
"Crayfish" herrings 20
Cream cheese pie 85
Creamed Baltic herring
casserole 55
Creamed mushrooms 30
Cucumber salad 55
Cured fillet of beef à la Mäkelä 50

Doughnuts, Finnish 85
Doughnuts, quick 11

Egg and rice filled pasties 84
Egg butter 84

Festive rowanberry parfait 26
Finnish coffee 88
Finnish doughnuts 85
Fish in aspic 55
Fish in paper 14
Fish pasty 57
Fish pie 57
Fresh-salted whitefish or
salmon 12

Fried salmon stakes 50

Gingerbread cookies 86
Glass master's herring 41
Graham rolls 80
Graham rusks 80
grahamkorput 80
grahamsämpylät 80
Ground meat and cabbage stew 43

Hamburger à la Lindström 54
hauki, täytetty 50
hernekeitto 43
Herring, Glass master's 41
Herring ice cream 48
Herring salad 41
Herrings with mustard dressing 55
Home-brewed beer 77
Home-made cheese 56

imelletty perunalaatikko 41
Inkoo porridge 65
Inkoon puuro 65

joulukinkku 40
joulutortut 42
Juice fool 72
juusto-sienipiirakka 84

kaalikääryleet 68
kaalilaatikko 43
kaalipiirakka 70
kahvia suomalaisittain 88
kala paperissa 14
kalahyytelö 55
kalakukko 57
kardemummakorput 92
Karelian pasties 84
Karelian stew 59
karjalanpaisti 59
karjalanpiirakat 84
karpalojäädyke 71
kauralastut 85
kaura-omenajälkiruoka 73
kaurasämpylät 80
keitetyt ravut 27
kesäkeitto 26
korvapuustit 85
kotijuusto 56
kotikalja 77
köyhät ritarit 73
Kulibiaka — salmon and rice
pasty 50
kurkkusalatti 55

lakkakääretorttu 86
lammaskaali 43
lanttulaatikko 41
Lapin taika 91
Lapland magic 91
lasimestarin silli 41
läskisoosi 69
lihakääryleet 34
lihakeitto 43

lihapiirakka 84
lihapullat 55
Lindströmin pihvi 54
Little cardamom rusks 92
Liver casserole 41
Liver pâté 54
lohi, ristiinnaulittu 16
lohi, tuoresuolattu 12
lohilaatikko 43
lohileikkeet, paistetut 50
lohipiirakka 50
lohitartar 46
lusikkaleivät 85
luumukermahyytelö 73
luumukiisseli 72

madekeitto 19
maksalaatikko 41
maksapasteija 54
mansikkatäytekakku 86
marjapuuro 72
marjasalaatti 73
Mashed potatoes 62
maustekakku 86
May Day cookies 11
Mead 10
Meat and cabbage stew 43
Meat pasty 84
Meatballs 55
mehukiisseli 72
Mother's apple cake 92
muna-riisipiirakka 84
munavoi 84
munkit 85
Mushroom relish 32
Mushroom salad 33
Mushrooms, creamed 30
Mustard dressing 13
mustikkakeitto 24
mustikkapiirakka 25
Mutton cabbage, baked

Nailed salmon 16
Nailed whitefish 16

Oat rolls 80
Oatmeal cookies 85
ohraleipä 80
ohrapuuro 67
ohukaiset 73
Old-fashioned roast veal 41
omenakakku, äidin 92
omenat, uunissa paistetut 73
Oven porridge from barley groats
or rice 67

paistetut ahvenet à la Havis
Amanda 48
paistetut lohileikkeet 50
paistetut omenat 73
paistetut silakat etikkaliemessä 20
pakastettu pihlajanmarjahilloke 26
Pancakes 73
Pancakes, Åland oven 60

pannukakku, Ahvenanmaan 60
Parainen gingerbread cookies 86
Paraisten piparkakut 86
patakukko 57
Pea soup 43
perunalaatikko, imelletty 41
perunapuuro 65
perunarieskat 82
perunasalaatti 76
perunasose 62
Pickled Baltic herrings 20
pihlajanmarjahilloke,
pakastettu 26
pihlajanmarjajäädyke 26
piimälimppu 79
pikamunkit 11
Pike, stuffed 50
piparkakut 86
Poor knights 73
Pork in gravy 69
Pork sausage soup 43
poronkäristys 62
Potato bread 82
Potato casserole, sweet-flavored 41
Potato pasties 82
Potato porridge 65
Potato salad 76
Prune cream 73
Prune fool 72
pulla 85

Quick doughnuts 11

rahkapiirakka 85
raparperihillo 26
raparperijuoma 26
rapusilakat 20
Raspberry Charlotte 73
ravut, keitetyt 27
Reindeer stew 62
Rhubarb drink 26
Rhubarb jam 26
riekko kermakastikkeessa 61
riimihärkää Mäkelän tapaan 50
ristiinnaulittu lohi 16
ristiinnaulittu siika 16
Roast veal, old-fashioned 41
Roll cake, cloudberry 86
Rowanberry parfait 26
Rowanberry pureé 26
ruisreikäleivät 79
Rutabaga casserole 41
Rye bread rounds 79

Salmon and rice pasty 50
Salmon casserole 43
Salmon, fresh-salted 12
Salmon, nailed 16
Salmon steak tartare 46
Salmon steaks, fried 50
sienimuhennos 30
sienipikkelsi 32
sienisalaatti 33
siika, ristiinnaulittu 16

siika, tuoresuolattu 12
silakat etikkaliemessä, paistetut 20
silakkapihvit 50
sillijäätelö 48
sillisalaatti 41
sima 10
sinappikastike 13
sinappisilakat 55
siskonmakkarakeitto 43
Snow grouse with creamy bird
sauce 61
Soft spice cake 86
Spawner perch à la Havis
Amanda 48
Spice cake, soft 86
Spoon cookies 85
Strawberry and cream cake 86
Stroganoff 69
Stuffed pike 50
Summer soup 26
Sweet-flavored potato casserole 41

täytetty hauki 50
tippaleivät 11
tuoresuolattu lohi 12
tuoresuolattu siika 12

uunikermasilakat 55
uunilahna 15
uunipuuro 67
uunissa paistetut omenat 73

vadelmacharlotta 73
vasikanpaisti 41
vatruskat 82
Veal birds 34
Vegetable beef soup 43
viili 67
voisilmäpullat 85
Vorschmack 64

Washington Eagle 90
Washingtonin kotka 90
Whipped berry porridge 72
Whitefish, fresh-salted 12
Whitefish, nailed 16

Weights

1 pound (lb) = 16 ounces = 453.6 grams (g)
1 ounce (oz) = 28.35 g
1 kilogram (kg) = 1000 g = 2 lbs 3 oz
100 g = 3.5 oz

Measures

1 US gallon = 4 liquid quarts = 3.785 liters (l)
1 liquid quart = 2 liquid pints = 9.5 deciliters (dl)
1 liquid pint = 16 US fl. oz. = 4.73 dl
1 cup = 8 US oz. = 2.37 dl
1 US fluid ounce (US fl. oz.) = 29.6 milliliters (ml)
1 quart (dry) = 1.1 l
1 liter = 10 dl = (more than) 2 pints
1 deciliter = (less than) 1/2 cup

Temperatures

Fahrenheit	Centigrade
268 °F	131 °C
350 °F	177 °C
375—400 °F	190—204 °C
450—500 °F	232—260 °C

Centigrade	Fahrenheit
100 °C	212 °F
200 °C	392 °F
250 °C	382 °F
300 °C	572 °F

Photographs:

ALKO 90, 91; Tim Bird 78; Elintarviketeollisuus 90, 91; Pekka Haraste/Fotoni 33, 34, 47, 93; Mikko Oksanen/Fotoni 9, 12, 15, 16, 18, 19, 25, 35, 36, 38, 39, 44, 45, 60, 61, 64; Ragnar Damström/Fotonokka/SOK; Arto Hallakorpi/Klikki 89; Mauri Korhonen 22, 23, 32, 33; Lehtikuva 63; Peter Lindholm/Lehtimiehet 76; Leipätoimikunta 81; Peter Lindholm 45; Seppo Konstig/Marttaliitto 31; Matkailun edistämiskeskus MEK 44, 57, 58, 59; Hannu Männynoksa 17; Raision Yhtymä 11, 77; Suomen Sokeri/Vaasan Mylly 42, 83, 86—87; Tapolan Palvaamo Oy 45; Valio Meijerien Keskusosuusliike 28—29, 40, 44, 49, 56, 66, 71, 74—75, 78; Yhtyneet Kuvalehdet 6—7, 52—53.

Cover photographs: Erkki Tuomala/Lehtikuvastudio LK, Leipätoimikunta, Matkailun edistämiskeskus MEK, Mikko Oksanen/Fotoni, Suomen Sokeri/Vaasan Mylly, Valio Meijerien Keskusosuusliike.

Drawings Pirjo Lausamo-Laine, Viljo Roine